W9-DAX-662

Remarriage in Midlife

Remarriage in Midlife

Plan It First, Make It Last

Helen Hunter

BAKER BOOK HOUSE
Grand Rapids, Michigan 49516

Copyright 1991 by
Baker Book House Company

Printed in the United States of America

Library of Congress Cataloging-in-Publication Data

Hunter, Helen
    Remarriage in midlife: plan it first, make it last/Helen Hunter.
      p. cm.
    Includes bibliographical references.
    ISBN 0-8010-4352-2
     1. Remarriage—United States. 2. Middle age—United States.
  3. Remarried persons—United States—Psychology. 4. Middle aged
persons—United States—Psychology. I. Title.
HQ1019.U6H86   1991
306.84—dc20   91–6686
                                                   CIP

Scripture quotations are from the New International Version, © 1978 by New York International Bible Society.

Contents

Dedication

This book is dedicated to Bud, my wonderful husband of ten years as of August 8, 1990. We're pressing on
toward another ten.

"Being confident of this, that he who began a good work
in [us] will carry it on to completion until the day of Christ
Jesus" (Phil. 1:6).

Acknowledgments

Thank you, my friend Dottie, you urged me to write this book way back in 1983. As we met, talked with one another, and became good friends, it became clear to us that marriage or remarriage in midlife has its own set of problems. Many couples face special hurts and problems that are certain not to be unique to the two of us. You encouraged me.

Thank you, Colleen, you helped me come to grips with my fear of reaching what I considered old age and never having done the one thing I wanted to do most—write full time. I did not want to be a sour sixty-year-old woman who said, "I will always wish I had done. . . . " You nudged me into obedience to God.

Thank you, Mary Lou, for reading and critiquing parts of my manuscript. I appreciate your comments and questions that led to my making this manuscript more readable.

Thank you to my church family for their prayers and encouragement.

I am grateful to all those men and women who allowed me to walk around in the private landscapes of their lives, who shared private and intimate thoughts and anecdotes with me. Their warmth and responses to my questions and their requests for a copy of the book (they were even more certain than I that the topic was important) gave me added encouragement and enthusiasm for the task.

Most of all I am thankful for my husband, Bud, for his love and support, for his reading and approval of the manuscript, and for his respect for my writing.

I thank God for my children, Steve and Sara, and for their love and acceptance; and my stepchildren, Jennifer, John, and Kevin, whom I love and have adopted in Christ. Without all of them there would be no book.

So in middle age, I attacked a book about middle age—remarrying when you are over forty.

1

Changes and Challenges in Midlife

I considered remarriage a closed issue. I was forty years old. I had been divorced for over ten years. Though there had been men in my life in dating relationships over the past years (and at least one of them had been important to me), I questioned my ability to have a successful marriage. In addition, I was, for the moment, thoroughly happy being alone with my children, with my budding career, and especially in my new and personal relationship with Jesus Christ.

My husband, however, says that he, at age forty-eight, desired a mate with whom he could spend his remaining years. He had "chased the elusive butterfly," but being unable to catch her had resigned himself to sitting and waiting for Providence to bring the butterfly to him. Shortly thereafter the pathways of our lives crossed. Little did I know I was to become the butterfly.

After our marriage however, the reality of a different set

of problems became apparent. Initially the difficulties seemed to be related mainly to children and stepchildren. Idealistic hopes for a melding of our two families of young adults were quickly dashed, not to even begin to be unraveled and resolved until we were nearly eight years into our marriage.

Interestingly enough, family counselors say, "If you can hang in there, usually things begin to iron out at about the seventh or eighth year."

I'm glad we hung in there!

The Middle Ages

For many men and women, celebrating the big fortieth or fiftieth birthday is exceedingly traumatic. Often our friends celebrate for us with black crepe paper and gifts that stress the fallen condition of our bodies. They see us as being "over the hill," even if we don't.

Once those of us in middle age come to grips with the labels, we are more or less ready to accept and enjoy some of the prerogatives that go with our age—influence, less responsibility, privacy and space, experience and maturity, maybe even wisdom. We have the freedom to come and go as we please. With some financial security we can rehearse retirement. In middle age we do not tend so much to future stargazing as we did in our twenties and thirties. Instead the here and now gets our major focus.

Putting an age label on true middle age is difficult. Some people are old at forty. Others are still young way into their sixties and seventies. I can't tell you how many times I've heard it—I know I have said it myself: Age is relative. You're only as old as you feel, or as you think you are.

"My husband was fifty-four when we married," said Joan. "But I think he was always old. He frequently said things like, 'If I live that long,' or 'I might not be alive next year.' He had a pessimistic attitude which affected his plans for the future."

On the other hand, Dottie at fifty-five said, "I wouldn't wish to be younger or turn back the clock. There are benefits gained through years of living. I've gotten to know myself better and have embraced life more. I am daring to do things I might not have done before. Because of my relationship with the Lord I have had the courage to live life to the fullest."

America is a graying nation. Medical skills and advances, including drugs, are keeping the elderly alive longer. Life expectancy is far greater than it was one hundred years ago. Still, men and women in middle age and older lose their life's mates to death, and more and more to divorce.

The statistics have changed drastically. Books and articles printed in the seventies refer to roughly one-fourth of all marriages ending in divorce. In their 1975 book, *Prime Time*, Bernice and Morton Hunt wrote: "Since one-fourth of *these* divorces occur after 15 or more years of marriage, there is something like a 1 in 16 chance that a husband and wife now entering middle age will end up in divorce court."[1]

In 1989 an alarming report was published by Teresa Castro Martin and Larry L. Bumpass, which said that "56 percent of recent first marriages would be likely to disrupt within 40 years of marriage."[2] It indicates the figure for broken marriages is over one-half, with some percentage of the divorces happening to men and women who have been bonded in marriage for up to forty years.

There are other sources, however, that disagree with the "50 percent-breakup" statistics. *Psychology Today* (September 1988) reported that analysts who divide the divorce rate by the marriage rate miscalculate. Statistics which reported 2.4 million marriages and 1.2 million divorces for 1981 failed to consider the fact that 50 million other marriages existed in that year. Therefore, the claim is that during 1981 only about 1 in 50 marriages ended in divorce.[3]

Whoever is right, there are still a good many men and women who find themselves alone in midlife, whether through death or divorce.

Neither men nor women have a corner on loneliness. Both sexes, when they find themselves alone in their middle years, often do not look forward to living the remainder of their lives alone, no matter what the statistics say.

Still others, having lived through loneliness within a marriage, understand that being alone and being lonely are two different things. One woman said, "I was alone and lonely sitting in the same room with my husband. At least when we were divorced and I was alone and lonely, it wasn't because I was being rejected by someone who was supposed to be my friend."

Remarriage: Is It for You?

Men and women come to remarriage in their middle years from many different places. Some have been widowed, some divorced. Some have dated several people since being single again. Maybe you are just now thinking about going out with someone special, but haven't dated since before you married the first time.

The "dating game" is difficult for older men and women alike. Sharing one's past and innermost thoughts with a new person is repugnant enough to some men and women to keep themselves from being available. To others, both divorced and widowed, the almost desperate need for companionship drives them into remarriage before they have given themselves the time and opportunity for grieving the loss of a previous mate and for closure of that relationship.

If you are thinking about remarriage, there are many things to ponder and consider—preferably *before* you tie the knot again.

Many times in remarriage you are faced with "Catch 22" situations. "Catch 22" comes from Joseph Heller's novel of World War II. It refers to a military regulation which said that concern for one's own safety in the face of real and immediate dangers was the process of a rational mind. This proof of sanity, however, only served to send the pilot out on further missions, which proved his craziness.

Remarriage can also be a "Catch 22." There will be no-win situations. Never underestimate the problems you will encounter which will need to be solved. Remarriage is dramatically different from first marriage. The issues are not similar to those confronting persons embarking on first marriage.

Putting the past behind you is an important first consideration. One of the reasons that action is so important is because the failure rate for remarriages is even higher than for first marriages. (Don't slam the book shut. Not yet.)

Remember the divorce statistics? You can plan ahead and choose not to be one of them. Statistics show that 75 of 100 divorced people remarry, and the tolerance level appears to go down. Of those 75 who remarry, 45 divorce again, making the remarriage failure rate 60 percent.

"We know that the recently severed, in their search for relief, sometimes sink into an alcohol-induced stupor, a period of promiscuity, a sea of pralines'n'cream," reported an article titled "I Do, I Do, I Do" by several *Newsweek* writers. "What we are just now finding out, though, is that there is a definite drug-of-choice among those unable to tolerate the aftershocks of a failed marriage or the prospect of a lonely life ahead. It is called remarriage."[4]

Ask people who have been married twice or three times, and they will agree they were not prepared for remarriage.

I don't want to make it sound like it's futile to try. Remarriage can work. Happily it does work. But that is exactly what it takes: *work.* And it is helpful if both parties are interested and involved in the work. Many others have walked before you through the uncharted territory of remarriage in midlife. Some have been overcome by the difficulties and have turned back. Others have suffered the pitfalls, persevered, and come out victorious. Learn from all of them.

Let Bygones Be Bygones

Preparation is crucial. Couples who marry on the rebound often go from the proverbial frying pan into the fire, perhaps refusing to face the issues or to prepare them-selves and their families. They did not take time to resolve old issues. You may be asking, What old issues?

Have you put the past behind you? Might you still har-bor a root of bitterness toward your previous mate? If you do, it will affect your new marriage relationship. And the effects can show in many different ways.

I can remember a time early in my remarriage when a word or a look from my husband would trigger a reaction in me. Was I responding to him? Sometimes I wasn't. I was playing old, tightly-wound "tapes" in my head from my previous marriage, the ghosts of marriage-past. I had a feel-ing of déjà vu—that this had happened before—and I thought I knew what would happen next. My defenses went up to protect myself. My husband experienced simi-lar flashes from his previous marriage, too.

"I counseled a woman once whose husband had given her a miserable life for fifteen years," writes Derek Prince, "then abandoned her and the children. I urged her to for-give him."

"'He's ruined fifteen years of my life,' she exclaimed indignantly, 'and you're asking me to forgive him?'"

"'Well, if you want him to ruin the rest of your life, too,' I replied, 'just keep on resenting him.' I reminded her that the one who resents suffers more than the one who is resented."[5]

Forgiving someone is a matter of your will, your decision to do it. The world tries to convince you that you have to have feelings before you have action. Wrong! You do not have to feel it. You have to will it.

Forgiving is not easy. In fact, our natural response to any deep or unfair hurt is to hate and to want to get even. Over the years I have said, jokingly, of course, "I don't get mad. I just get even." Unfortunately, that is how many people feel when they have been injured. They return injury for injury. They hate the hurter.

Many times I thought I simply could not forgive people for what they had said or done to me. You know what? I could have. I chose not to. Have you ever said, "I have to work it through. It may take some time before I can forgive you for how you have hurt me."

God can give us the willingness to forgive. We can be ever thankful that he is a forgiving God who does not hold out his forgiveness until he has "worked it through." With his help we can forgive—again and again, if that is what it takes.

Only through prayer, God's grace, and our own determination to leave the past behind can we hope to live successfully in the present. Our attitude should be like the apostle Paul's: "But one thing I do: Forgetting what is behind and straining toward what is ahead, I press on toward the goal to win the prize for which God has called me heavenward in Christ Jesus" (Phil. 3:13–14).

It doesn't do any good to hold onto the past. My wise husband says, "Yesterday is a cancelled check. Today is cash. Tomorrow is a promissory note."

Feelings about the Ex-spouse

How will you handle a meeting with the person who previously shared your intended mate's life?

Both Bud and I have children from our previous marriages. Our previous spouses are the children's parents, and nothing will change that. They were, in our opinion, worthy of our consideration, so we determined to make our considerateness of them work. Some readers will find it difficult to believe this (sometimes I even pinch myself to be sure it's true), but both Bud and I have caring and considerate relationships with our previous spouses and, perhaps even more amazingly, with one another's previous spouses.

Once when Bud's children were all home at Easter, we invited their mother to come for breakfast so she could see them all together. My children's father has been welcomed in our home on several occasions.

However, I am keenly aware of some remarried families in which previous spouses receive only curses and negative responses from their old spouses. If this sounds familiar to you, you probably have not dealt with your feelings about the ex-spouse.

We are aware that with only two of our five children married, the potential is good there will be other opportunities such as weddings to be thrown together with ex-mates. Then there will be shared grandchildren. We do hope, as much as is in our power, that those times will be pleasant.

A recent newspaper column expressed a woman's desire to be included in her stepdaughter's wedding after having been married to her father for twelve years. She had not been included in the invitations. She wasn't asked to stand in the receiving line. She was having trouble with what she perceived as rejection, but did not want to do something that would spoil the young woman's wedding day.

The columnist's reply, I thought, was a little harsh, but accurate in theory. Since the girl made an obvious choice to leave her stepmother out of the wedding it was suggested that the best wedding gift she could give was her absence.

Everyone knows someone whose marriage ceremony was ruined by angry parents or stepparents. Be determined that you will not participate in such madness.

Consider that Christ loves our previous spouses and died for their sins, too. Our responsibility is to express his love, no matter what.

What May Go Wrong in Your Remarriage

A friend reminded me of an old song many of us sang during our teens: "Second verse same as the first. It could get better, but it's gonna get worse." While I think it was sung to warn listeners about another verse of poor singing, it can apply to remarriage. Everything that went wrong the first time can still go wrong. And more.

Counselors' files are full of statistics which prove that individuals and couples experience the same problems in their second marriages as in their unsuccessful first. We often select mates with the same personalities and characteristics as our first mates. Many times the traits of the other person play into our own character weaknesses or defects. Friends of the first couple will often comment on how the new mate even looks like the first one.

Before you take the trip down the aisle the second time, take the time to figure out what went wrong in your first marriage. Profit from your mistakes, learning from them to do better. Most people learn more from their mistakes than they do from their successes. It is never too late to begin to do what is right.

What Is God's Plan for Your Life?

Are you running ahead of God? In the blush of new love, feelings race pell-mell ahead of logic. Both men and women are prone to think they know the mind of God when it comes to male-female relationships, particularly the ones they are involved in. Since God was the designer of marriage, and he has not changed his mind or his instructions, you might want to ask yourself some pertinent questions: If God is in this decision to remarry, if it is his idea, won't it last? Must I hurry? What is the pressure to hurry into remarriage?

One woman said, "From my human perspective it was nice not to have to struggle economically." A man said, "I hated the courting business. I think I married her so I wouldn't have to always be 'on.'" One woman described how her gentleman friend pursued her, inviting her to dinner several nights each week, taking her to movies and generally being the man-about-town. Finally she agreed to marry him, believing him to be an interesting and exciting person. After the marriage he didn't want to go anywhere.

Are you in a hurry for a physical relationship? But you want it to be within the bounds of matrimony? Some of you are incurable romantics, believing the myths perpetrated in love songs.

What Is a Successful Remarriage?

A successful remarriage first of all needs God in the center and then two healthy people who are emotionally free. Emotionally healthy people know who they are and what they are looking for in a mate, and make careful and prayerful decisions for themselves.

There are other pros and cons in a midlife remarriage. The pesky cons are likely to cause problems unless the couple is willing to address them before remarriage. We shall address these things in detail in following chapters.

What will be the foundation of your remarriage? Will it be based on Christian principles? What other values do you share? Disagree about?

Greater financial security may be yours simply because you have been with a career or at a company a long time and have worked up to a high salary or hold an executive position. Or you may still be paying alimony or child support for your previous family. Have you talked about that? Have you talked about other money issues such as insurance, wills, inheritance, personal possessions?

Are there grandchildren? You may need to make a decision about whether or not you want to become "built-in" baby sitters for your grandchildren. You may decide these are your years of freedom, freedom to get acquainted, travel, and make friends with your contemporaries. It is vitally important that you have time to develop intimacy with one another.

In midlife we feel fairly secure about our places in the world. Our children are taking care of themselves. "Whew," we say, wiping our brows, when they receive their college diplomas or get the jobs that will give them security into the future. Often it is then we realize that our own parents are aging and in need of our help and advice. Caught on the cusp between youth and old age, we do not know when accidents or illness might strike in our own lives. Have you talked about health issues?

Will your new family be made up of children from two

marriages? Will you have children of your own? Don't laugh. People over forty do bear children; many of them are called mistakes, change-of-life babies, or midlife children.

If children are not already out of the nest, how soon will they be? Have you talked about that? Perhaps you have ushered your children down the aisle in their own marriages. They may even have families of their own. You may expect to be unburdened by the issues that so often weigh down a stepfamily. But problems in this area are not necessarily simpler. Often they are more complex.

Do you have a built-in extended family, previous in-laws, or grandchildren? Couples marrying in midlife sometimes feel they are on "relationship overload" with too many people to get to know and care about, too many different personalities to relate to, too many people to buy gifts for, too many hurts from previous relationships to be involved in (or excluded from).

Bud and I were having dinner with our close friends, Ann and Larry, between Christmas and New Year 1988. The conversation, as always, was easy and unpretentious.

"I've spent several days wondering why this Christmas was so much better than last year," Bud said. "Last year was so awful anything would have been an improvement. I really enjoyed this one."

"What do you think it was?" Ann asked.

"I think," Bud continued, "it was the lack of conflict. All of the kids who were home actually wanted to be there. They seemed to be enjoying one another, too."

Needless to say, I was pleased, too. I truly am thankful we hung in there.

2

Help from the Top

I can remember several times when I recognized that my life was out of control. I needed help.

I seemed propelled to the church for counsel and, hopefully, an answer to my problems. That was remarkable because I had not been close to the church. I didn't consider myself a religious person. Today I wonder if I went to the church to hear someone validate aloud what I was hearing in the secret places of my soul—that God was patiently waiting for my turn from immorality and selfishness to trust him with the direction of my life.

It is tempting to operate under the assumption that all people want valid answers and good help for their questions and problems. But I have come to realize that everyone has a different tolerance for pain and some people have to hurt a bunch before they will give up and cry out for help.

Because I reached that initial point many years ago and because I now long to grow as a Christian and be a whole and healthy person I have to be careful not to assume that everyone else feels the way I do.

We do not know why God allows some people to recog-

nize him early in their life through the beauty of his creation, or through the miracle of a healing, or simply by recognizing God's grace in the daily interactions with one another.
Many people with whom I talk have had to be brought to
their knees through pain, loss of family or job, or other catas-
trophes before they recognize their need for a Savior.

On a recent Sunday one of the senior high boys in my
church shared his thankfulness for an event that happened
over a year and a half earlier. His three front teeth had been
punched out by some bullies who simply didn't like him.
The young man related from the perspective of time that
God had gotten his attention through the pain and the
unfairness. Though losing his teeth would not have been
his choice, he is thankful for his relationship with God. At
age seventeen!

As I'm writing this chapter, I ponder, is it fair to assume
that you, the reader, are looking for valid answers right
where you are, at the beginning of or well into midlife,
contemplating remarriage, and eager to see what others say
before you make your final decision?

Or perhaps you are reading this after you have remarried. Do you wish this information had been available to
you earlier? Hangeth thou in there!

Help from the Church

I feel fairly comfortable in saying I do believe most pastors do not favor divorce. Still it is important to know that
because of the fallen human condition, pastors and
Christian counselors sometimes give advice which goes
against God's will for our lives. You may recognize deep
inside yourself that such advice is leaving an unmet need.

One woman expressed the lack of peace that she felt in
her heart when her Christian counselor advised her to
leave her noncommunicative husband. The counselor
dubbed the marriage dead—hopeless. She, however, sought
God in prayer and decided that the advice was wrong for
her and she communicated her decision to the counselor.

The counselor may have thought the reasons for his recommendations were good, and in other situations they might have been. This woman knew, though, that with previous relationship problems her method of dealing was to run. Now since she was a Christian, she wanted to stand firm and resolve the problems, trusting that God would teach both her and her husband that their marriage could, and would, be salvaged.

During the searching times when I was driven to "the church" for help, I believe God was drawing me to himself. Inside of me was that God-shaped vacuum that nothing could fill except the Spirit of God. God wants to be first to give us direction through his Word and through prayer. When a pastor, a counselor, or respected Christian gives us counsel, it always needs to be measured by the truth of the Scriptures.

Anyone who takes advice which abandons the standards of God and his Word is on sinking sand. If infidelity and lack of commitment to marriage vows are not openly discouraged, then somehow they are vicariously encouraged.

Jane, a remarried Christian, related that when she went to a Christian counselor her heart was hardened against further hurt from her husband who continued to be involved in extramarital affairs. While she did not want her marriage to fail, still she wanted to get out of it to protect herself from more hurt. Her counselor helped her see her unwillingness to let go and completely trust God with her fears, her husband and his behavior, and the outcome of their marriage.

"My counselor told me I must trust God, that I should tell my husband his affairs were not okay with me, that he would need to agree to submit to counseling, and that we might need a time of separation," said Jane. "But I also told him I intended to honor my vows of marriage—no matter what." Jane got sound advice. Unfortunately, her husband chose not to meet her even halfway, and instead instituted divorce proceedings.

Another woman said that because of the time she spent in counseling, her pastor knew that her marriage was of the highest priority. "When my husband went ahead and sued me for divorce, I felt soiled and unworthy," she said. "And I was concerned about how my church would receive me."

Though the church sometimes falls short of Christ-like compassion, in this case her pastor assured her there would be no problems.

Later this woman gave her testimony before her church and told of God's sufficiency in the midst of her pain and sorrow at her failed marriage. The people responded with warmth and love. That is the way it should be. The church is the very place where hurting persons should expect a sense of stability and security in the midst of their pain.

The world's philosophy, "If it doesn't work out we can always get a divorce" has, unfortunately, penetrated the walls of the church. The stick-to-itiveness which made marriage partners stick it out through thick and thin not that many years ago does not have to lose its adhesive qualities in today's marriages.

Those of us who *are* the church however, must be careful not to judge a man or woman whose mate has instituted divorce to marry another. Often the person is already suffering from rejection by a dearly loved spouse. Surely more rejection would not be kind. Divorced or separated people do not suddenly become inadequate or imperfect. They are hurt and need the blessing of our love.

Although neither my previous husband nor I were more than token church attenders, I sinned in getting divorced. My sin was in looking only for what would be good for me. I lived a completely self-consumed existence (I cannot say life, because it was void of anything that would speak of life from a Christian's point of view—joy, peace, love). I wanted only what was best for me, and according to my set of values, and if anything interfered with that mindset, I rejected it.

I can also tell you with all the certainty of God's holy Word backing me up that since I confessed my previous divorce as sin in God's sight, he was faithful and just and forgave me that sin and cleansed me from all unrighteousness (1 John 1:9). I am forgiven and clean! I am sorry for those things that were part of my life before Christ, selfish deeds and actions that grieved my Lord. I am also fully aware of the emotional pain and the problems my choices have caused my children.

On an up note, I am thankful God's Word further confirms that "If anyone is in Christ, he is a new creation; the old has gone, the new has come" (2 Cor. 5:17)! The old stuff is gone. Behind me. Finished.

"Those who challenge the right of such repentant believers to a completely new start in life are in danger of ignoring the warning given to Peter in Acts 10:15: 'Do not call anything impure that God has made clean,'" said Derek Prince.[1]

That new start in life, however, does not erase what has gone before. The facts of our previous life are still there, and there is often much hurt to be forgiven, changes to be made in thinking and behavior, restoration to be made in family members. Never let it be said that divorce does not leave wreckage. It does.

What Does the Church Say About Remarriage?

I interviewed several divorced people who said they felt the church considered them second-class citizens. Some churches did not permit them to have positions of leadership because of their divorces. Their question always was, "If God can forgive me, why can't my church?"

Author Delores Kuenning in her book *Helping People Through Grief* tells of Nell, who being divorced after twenty-one years of marriage described it as "worse than death."

"My husband and I were both very active in church," she said. "I felt terribly let down by the church during our divorce. It seemed as though my church friends were unable to perceive me as a person in pain. Churches are very couple-oriented, so immediately I felt out of place. My social life literally ended."[2]

Another woman in Kuenning's book whose husband died very young described her condition as "now single, a misfit living in a coupled world."[3]

As I have watched men and women who have been involved in divorce, I wonder if the church misses the distinction between the guilty and the innocent party. Are both parties to a divorce guilty? Should they both be treated the same? Derek Prince commented in his book *God Is a Matchmaker* that it would make as much sense to suggest that both parties to a robbery are guilty and should be treated the same.[4]

"Many divorced-remarried persons . . . suffer endless moral cruelty," writes Guy Duty in his book *Divorce and Remarriage*. "They are accepted into the membership, admitted to the Holy Communion, but put under the moral penalty of not being allowed to sing in the choir, teach a Sunday school class, or perform other services in the church —which leaves them in the shadow of adultery. They are half-saint and half-adulterer."[5]

On another front, men and women should remember that the church has scriptural qualifications for elders and pastors. Those who do not fit those guidelines need not feel guilty. Groups and organizations, too, have established rules regarding their membership or leadership. I remember how hurt I felt when I learned that because I had been divorced I might not lead a particular Bible study. In praying about it, though, I recognized their right to have rules. It was my responsibility to abide by the rules and realize that the rules were not set against me.

My intention is not that this book be a theological tome. However, it is not difficult to believe that the grace of God is sufficient to cover the sin of divorce, the same as any other sin.

I do not desire to prove or disprove Scripture's position on divorce or remarriage. For nearly two thousand years there has been disagreement on this subject, and it would be time and effort wasted for me, a layperson, to try to solve it. But I do make the assertion that once divorce has happened there is a sizable chance for a remarriage. Since statistics show that 60 percent of second marriages fail, a good case can be made for working to better that percentage within Christ's church.

Unfortunately, the erosion of the world has become all too real in the church. Suffice it to say that (1) Christians get divorced; (2) people accept Christ after they've been divorced; and (3) men and women from both categories do remarry.

Wounded people do not need to be kicked when they are down. They need healing and answers to the questions they are asking—answers that will help them to be better prepared for a successful remarriage.

James 2:12–13 gives us good guidance: "Speak and act as those who are going to be judged by the law that gives freedom, because judgment without mercy will be shown to anyone who has not been merciful. Mercy triumphs over judgment!"

What Does Scripture Say About Remarriage?

I recommend Edward G. Dobson's book *What the Bible Really Says About Marriage, Divorce and Remarriage* as a good resource. He gives a careful and loving explanation of Scripture, leaving the reader with the certainty of God's love and forgiveness.

He concludes after his chapter "Divorce and the Teachings of Moses," from his study of Deuteronomy 24, that "God commands permanence in marriage. God permits divorce. God permits remarriage."[6]

Then what about the New Testament?

Did Jesus give a new teaching about divorce in the New Testament that supersedes the Old Testament? Carefully read Jesus' teachings from the Sermon on the Mount in Matthew 5. In verses 17 to 32 alone note how many times Jesus refers to Old Testament teachings.

"Jesus is not nullifying the Old Testament Law of divorce

any more than He voided the Old Testament Law on murder and adultery," says Dobson. "He was reminding them of the intent of the Law—to enhance the permanence and fidelity of marriage. He was emphasizing the lack of commitment to marriage."[7]

What about remarriage? In Matthew 19:9 Jesus allowed an exception: "I tell you that anyone who divorces his wife, except for marital unfaithfulness, and marries another woman commits adultery."

"If Christ had intended to prohibit remarriage, He probably would have made it much clearer than He did in this passage," says Dobson. "In both the Old Testament and the prevailing viewpoints in Christ's day, remarriage was always permitted based upon an appropriate bill of divorcement. Consequently, the people to whom Christ was giving this teaching on divorce presupposed the legitimacy of remarriage after proper grounds for divorce."[8]

In 1 Corinthians 7:27–28 Paul says, "Are you married? Do not seek a divorce. Are you unmarried? ("Art thou loosed from a wife?" renders the KJV.) Do not look for a wife. But if you do marry, you have not sinned; and if a virgin marries, she has not sinned. But those who marry will face many troubles in this life, and I want to spare you this."

"Who is being married in verse 28? There are only three options," says Dobson. "Paul could be talking to someone who has been divorced, a widow or a widower, or a virgin. I do not believe Paul was talking to virgins, because in the next clause he addresses virgins directly. So Paul is talking to people who have lost their mates through death or divorce."[9]

Paul's footnote in verse 28 "nevertheless such shall have trouble" (KJV) underscores the fact that people who remarry after divorce have a more difficult time in their second marriage. Why should that be?

I believe it is because so many people bring the same old problems into their new marriages, not having taken the time to resolve them before remarriage. That's what this book is about essentially—to give those men and women who are looking at the possibility of remarriage ideas and resources to prepare themselves for the happiness and contentment that can be theirs—happiness that is based in the truth of Scripture and a relationship with Jesus Christ as Lord and Savior.

But That Doesn't Apply to Me!

Many people will say that the above teachings do not apply to them, because they began their relationships with Jesus Christ since their divorce. Or there may be readers who still do not have that relationship with the Savior.

Perhaps it is timely to pause here and ask if you want another marriage that is centered in self, in possessions, in careers, or in any other "thing" that sets itself up as an idol against God.

We've already discussed God's ideal for marriage: It is to be permanent—one man, one woman, one lifetime—and the truth that if we have been divorced and have asked forgiveness, we are forgiven through Jesus Christ.

God still hates divorce and the sin that leads to it. And divorce is still frowned on by the Christian church. But Christians are being divorced—like it or not—and they are remarrying. Add to those numbers men and women who have come to Christ for salvation after their divorces or the death of their mates, or after their remarriages. The numbers are staggering.

Divorce has been easy to get with no-fault laws. Society has said religious beliefs are no longer important. Christians may have bought into the lie that "everyone is doing it; it must be okay." Divorce has become socially acceptable. But for the sake of a position on which to base this book, may we agree that if we remarry, it will be a lifetime commitment—till death do us part?

We shall plan it first and make it last.

No one, least of all Christians, should go into a remarriage with the idea that "if it doesn't work out we'll get a divorce." It will take a commitment on the part of both parties to make the remarriage work. The problems couples will encounter in a remarriage are very real. Most people who are involved in remarriage in midlife will attest to the fact that it takes a lot of work.

So if you have not already committed your life to Jesus Christ as Savior, perhaps right now would be a good time. Prayer, sincerely meant in your heart, will open the door to eternal life in Jesus Christ. It will also demand of you obedience to God and his Word, the Bible. Don't take this step of faith lightly. Receiving Jesus Christ as your Lord and Savior is the biggest and most important step of your life.

Prayer of Salvation

Lord Jesus, I need you. Thank you for dying on the cross for my sins. I open the door of my life and receive you as my Savior and Lord. Forgive me of my sins and give me eternal life. I step off the throne of my life and give you control. Make me the kind of person you want me to be. I thank you and give you the praise and the glory. Amen.

You are a born-again Christian.

Do you not know that the wicked will not inherit the kingdom of God? Do not be deceived: Neither the sexually immoral nor idolaters nor adulterers nor male prostitutes nor homosexual offenders nor thieves nor the greedy nor drunkards nor slanderers nor swindlers will inherit the kingdom of God. And that is what some of you *were* [emphasis mine]. But you were washed, you were sanctified, you were justified in the name of the Lord Jesus Christ and by the Spirit of our God (1 Cor. 6:9-11).

What Does Scripture Say About Marriage?

God is always interested and wants to be involved in our lives, even in the minutest details. We should depend on him to give us guidance in our selection of a lifetime mate.

"God was definitely involved in our marriage plans," said Samantha. "He had confirmed the rightness of the remarriage several times, sanctifying us together for ministry."

Ask yourself these most important questions for Christians remarrying: Is the person I love and want to marry a Christian? Does he share my spiritual values? What are her beliefs?

If you are coming to this book as a Christian—whether you have been walking with the Lord for a long time, or whether you just prayed the prayer of salvation—you will want to know what God says about Christian men and women marrying unbelievers.

I cannot stress long and hard enough the importance of not glossing over this area and being willing to accept less than what God has planned for you. Many remarriages founder on the rocks of discontent when one of the couple has a personal relationship with Jesus Christ and the other does not.

"I knew when I married again I wanted a man who attended church and believed in God," said Joan, "but what I didn't know was that going to church did not translate into being a Christian." Joan married a man who "religiously" prayed and "religiously" attended church, but who in reality had no relationship with Christ. While Joan grew as a new Christian, she became aware that she was unequally yoked, though she had not been taught the truths from Scripture before remarrying.

Her advice is repeated over and over by men and women who have married or remarried someone who did not believe: "Don't do it! My strong trust and belief in God did not set well with my husband. He considered me to be a Jesus freak and ridiculed my faith, the time I spent with the Lord, my friends who were Christians. It was unpleasant to say the least."

"I don't believe it was God's plan for me to marry John," said another woman. "But I believe he *allowed* me to go ahead. And there were many problems because of our differences in belief." This woman is divorced for the second time. If she had it to do over again, she would not have married an unbeliever.

How many other men and women, do you suppose,

have remarried believing that because their prospective spouses attended church with them they were believers?

In the warmth of a new relationship, attending church together is fairly easy. It is even easy to promise that church attendance will be an important part of the remarriage.

Some men or women reading this will admit to thinking, "As soon as we marry and live under the same roof, as soon as he (or she) sees how real Christ is in my life, then he'll make a real commitment to Jesus Christ." The underlying belief here is: I can change him (her).

Being Equally Yoked Is Not Just for Oxen

I never cease to be amazed at how God directs people where they need to be at specific times. Once a young woman came to my home to talk about Successful Living, the Christian book business/ministry in which I have been involved for nearly ten years. She was planning marriage and wanted to have work in the new community where they would move.

"Is your fiancé a Christian?" I asked, more boldly than usual.

She carefully stepped away from the question and replied, "He goes to church."

Coincidentally (God-incidentally?) I had that morning read a short story in a Christian magazine about a young woman who had married an unbeliever, had questioned her fiancé's relationship with Christ, but had plunged ahead and married him. Immediately he stopped attending church. He stopped even pretending to hunger for the things of God. Instead he ridiculed his new wife's beliefs. He had purposely deceived her.

I shared the story with Laurie. She thanked me and left. I did not see her for several years and when I did, I couldn't remember where we had met.

"You told me about Successful Living. Then you told me not to marry an unbeliever," she reminded me.

"Did you?"

"No, for once I took someone's advice," she said with a bright smile. "Thank God, I did!"

One reading of 2 Corinthians 6:14–18 will give you God's plan and his direction for your marriage.

> Do not be yoked together with unbelievers. For what do righteousness and wickedness have in common? Or what fellowship can light have with darkness? What harmony is there between Christ and Belial? What does a believer have in common with an unbeliever? What agreement is there between the temple of God and idols? For we are the temple of the living God. As God has said: "I will live with them and walk among them, and I will be their God, and they will be my people."

The literal Greek translation of the term *yoked together* means "to be paired with another kind, coupled to someone of a different sort."[10]

The yoke is an unfamiliar piece of equipment in this day and age, though in Bible times it was commonplace. Beasts of burden wore the yoke to create balance between them. The wooden frame kept their heads in place and kept them walking side by side. The yoke made them a team. If one of the oxen pulled ahead, the yoke chafed both of their necks. If one lagged behind, the same was true.

When you reconsider being unequally yoked with a mate who is not walking in the Spirit with you, it gives a picture of imbalance. Pain and chafing result as one spouse wants to move ahead, growing in Christ, while the other has no interest.

Once a couple is married, though, the yoke is in place, and the believing partner will be drawn against his or her will in directions and toward things which may be abhorrent. It will chafe. It will be difficult to walk as a team.

One of the early love letters from Ed McCully to Marilou Hobolth, which was published in Elisabeth Elliot's book *Through Gates of Splendor,* always touches my heart. It reads:

> I'm praying definitely for two things: first, that the Lord will give us wisdom in our relationship—even in the business of

letter writing. Second, that as long as we've got anything to do with each other, that each of us will be an influence upon the other for closer fellowship with the Lord. I don't mean that we'll be *preaching* to each other—but just that our attraction for each other will be a means of attracting us more to the Lord. I know that's the way you feel too.[11]

If the person you are seeing is not influencing for good your relationship with the Lord Jesus, then stop. Do you really think you're going to change him? Win her to the Lord later? Marrying with this idea would be to willfully disobey God. Disharmony will be the result. The disobedient Christian is joining a child of God with a child of Satan. An unholy alliance is thereby created, which is what Paul has described in 2 Corinthians 6 when he asks, "What harmony is there between Christ and Belial?"

The persons who go ahead with remarriage plans knowing the truth from God's point of view will reap what they sow. There will be consequences for their decisions: ideological conflicts, choices between the Lord and the loved spouse, oppression, and lack of meaningful communication between the partners. Is it worth that?

Deep discussions before remarriage are in order. Does he have a testimony? Can a date be pinpointed when she was saved? Is he or she vague about a relationship with Jesus? Beware!

Do you ever pray together? Do you set godly examples for each other? Do you build up each other in spiritual matters? Is there disagreement in spiritual things?

After settling completely the issue of the condition of one's heart toward Jesus Christ and the resulting relationship with him, the door will be open to discuss the items that could be problems in remarriage.

3

From Wreckage to Renewal

Are you taking time today, Helen?"

"For what?"

"To deal with your anger," said Dave, the peer-group counselor.

"I don't understand why you keep pushing me on this anger business," I snapped. "I AM NOT ANGRY!"

"Look at your coffee cup, Helen," he replied softly.

The cup's edge had been chewed off while I listened to someone else work on his anger in our group therapy session. Dave saw this and believed we had touched the tip of my own anger.

That day, and for several sessions to follow, I began to deal with anger—anger I had carried in a huge invisible bag slung over my shoulder. I had lugged it for years (some of it for up to twenty years). Most, though, had been recently piled on the top because of my divorce and the unfair treatment I received from men—my ex-husband, significant others, egocentric bosses.

The bag was so full the anger had begun to leak out, dribbling onto unsuspecting people, such as a poor shoe salesman who brought out a 9B instead of the 9AA I had requested.

Anger, unresolved, was tucked deep in my stomach, birthing a painful ulcer. Anger deep in my diaphragm hampered a deep breath. I sighed a lot. My posture, normally erect and proud, was gone, replaced by stooped shoulders that yelled, "Defeated! Victim!"

Have You Been Hurt?

When middle age people have a marriage suddenly broken by death or divorce, they feel they are half of what they should be. They are half of what they are accustomed to and they want to be in a couple again—one flesh, not half-flesh.

People who have lost mates, whether to death or divorce, are angry. And they grieve. It takes time to heal from the loss of an important relationship. Books written on loss show that people suffer pain and loneliness after a major move to another city. They have lost their friends, close business associates, neighbors. Anyone who has ever embarked on a new adventure and left a loved one behind knows well the feelings of loneliness and loss.

Those feelings are magnified several times in death and divorce. "Divorce is the psychological equivalent of a triple coronary bypass," writes Mary Kay Blakely. "After such a monumental assault on the heart, it takes years to amend all the habits and attitudes that led up to it."[1]

They must be dealt with, however, before a man and woman can successfully embark on a remarriage.

If, on the other hand, you think you have not experienced loss, hurt, anger, or some form of emotional trauma because of your divorce or death of your mate, is there a possibility you are suppressing your feelings?

One counselor spoke of a woman he had worked with who appeared to have a good Christian marriage. She said they didn't quarrel. The home was peaceful. The truth, however, was that there were problems and hurts repressed inside her and long forgotten. Suddenly one day there was an explosion as they poured into her conscious mind. The storm of hate and bitterness was volcanic.

A first step is to be truthful and admit you are hurting. Don't put your feelings in bags and strap them shut for safekeeping (my friend Lonnett calls it "gunny sacking"). God is merciful and will heal the emotional wounds from your previous marriage or from the death of a loved one.

Look at Sara and Sue, hypothetical friends who arranged to share an apartment. They had looked for just the right place together and agreed on what they would rent. They had talked openly about their expectations of one another. They had even discussed what each of them would bring to the apartment to make it their home.

But on moving day, Sue came dragging twenty extra pieces of baggage and left it all setting in the middle of the living room floor. Sara was undeniably dismayed.

"What is all that stuff?" she asked.

"That's my old baggage," Sue replied, "all of the stuff I have accumulated over the years. I always drag it with me everywhere I go."

"But what are you going to do with it?" Sara asked.

"I keep it because I need it. The bags are full of memories . . .," she began to look a little sheepish when she realized that Sara wanted to know more, " . . . and some hurts. And resentments. Bitterness. Okay, expectations and disappointments."

It's plain to see no roommate would want bags and bags of hurts, resentments, bitterness, expectations, and disappointments cluttering up her home. Wouldn't it seem reasonable to expect Sue to go through her bags and sort them—letting go of those things she will have no use for, giving up items that will continue to cause her pain, and making scrapbooks of those pleasant memories she wants to keep?

It is the same with relationships in a remarriage. While

it is often true that the emotional divorce lags behind the legal one, we easily carry into our new relationships the emotional baggage of unresolved issues from important past relationships. How much better to come unencumbered, free from past hauntings.

It is unrealistic to imagine that there will never be painful memories from the past in a remarriage. Each of us is the sum total of all the pains and joys that have come into our lives through people, places, things, and circumstances. But we are also in control of what part the gnarly things from the past will play in our lives today.

Stopping the Blame Games

Is it fair to assume that by the time we have reached our middle age we should be mature—not only physically but, hopefully, emotionally? Emotional maturity is taking responsibility for our behavior, thoughts, words, and deeds. Simply put, it means making choices and being willing to accept their consequences.

Daily I meet men and women who have grown old but who have not grown up, who are still infants in their thinking. How sad to watch a middle-aged man pitch a fit like a small child, to hear an older woman blame someone for the choice she has just made and which backfired.

It's time to stop the blame games and grow up.

Other-directed Blame Games

After my divorce my attitude was, "Everyone wants to get me. Why me? Poor me." I assessed blame to others for many of the problems in my life. One day I was ticking off the mental list of grievances done against me. In every instance there was a common denominator. It was I. "Am I always right?" I asked myself. "Are others always wrong?"

Would a remarriage at this point in my life have been successful? God bless the poor man who might have tried it. It would have been doomed because of my bags full of anger.

The answers to my own questions, truthfully, were

shocking! For the first time in many years I could look at the choices I had made (no one forced me into making them) and take the total responsibility for my own life. The answers to my own questions changed not only my behavior but also my life.

God-directed Blame Games

If you were the wounded person in a divorce, or if you suddenly lost a loved one to death, rather than blaming others for your predicament you may be angry at God and blaming him for the circumstances of your life.

God is not to blame. That is the first hurt you need to put to rest. God did not make this hurt happen to you. God is God. "'For my thoughts are not your thoughts, neither are your ways my ways,' declares the LORD. 'As the heavens are higher than the earth, so are my ways higher than your ways and my thoughts than your thoughts'" (Isa. 55:8–9).

God sometimes allows things we will not understand on this side of heaven. This is where faith becomes real, "being sure of what we hope for and certain of what we do not see" (Heb. 11:1).

Self-directed Blame Games

Those who are the "innocent" parties in divorce, in addition to other-blaming have a tendency to be hard on themselves. "If only I had kept the house and the children cleaner." "If only I had been more available to him sexually." "If only I had included her in my nightly golf games, she might not have left me." (It's true, she might not have.)

"If only" thinking is unproductive and will not usually restore a broken marriage. It certainly does not bring back a deceased loved one.

On the other hand, it is true that there are usually two sides to every story, and you may have been partially or wholly to blame for the breakup. Maybe you were the "theologically guilty" party; let's say you *did* break God's law by divorcing, maybe even by remarrying.

Is that unforgivable in God's eyes? No, the only unforgivable sin is rejection of Jesus Christ. God's grace covers your sin, and relief is offered through Jesus who died to satisfy God's judgment on your sin. If God accepted the sacrifice of Christ as payment for your sin, won't you? God is a forgiving God and will restore you to fellowship with him once you have confessed your wrongs. Receive his forgiveness. It's greater than your sin.

"What shall we say, then? Shall we go on sinning so that grace may increase? By no means!" (Rom. 6:1, 2a).

Remodeling Required

Often under the pile of anger, whether at another person, at God, or self-directed, is a tender and vulnerable person who has been desperately hurt. One woman had hung onto her hurts since her divorce eight years earlier. As she talked about them, they sounded like cherished friends. She hugged them to herself. They were her protection, her defense against more hurts.

However, to go on hurting emotionally long after an injury takes place is like slow suicide. You can make a choice to take control of the hurts. You can decide to let go of them.

Remodeling requires the removal of old pain and hurts before "The Carpenter" can replace them with his grace and peace.

Dale Galloway says it well in his book *Dream a New Dream.* He writes:

> When God made us, what a marvelous combination he put within us in giving us the capacity to think and feel. This gives us the potential for ecstasy on one hand and agony on the other. Being made as we are, and our world being what it is, there is no person alive who will pass through life without suffering some emotional pain. To go a step further, I seriously doubt there is anyone who lives who can escape being unjustly treated at some time by another person.[2]

Do you believe God is sovereign? That he has supreme power in each of our lives? Have you accepted the truth that God is a forgiving God? The death of Jesus Christ on the cross was enough to cover even your sins.

Psalm 55:22 says: "Cast your cares on the LORD and he will sustain you; he will never let the righteous fall."

Then how about giving him your pain and your cares? Are you willing? Jesus was hurt that we might be healed. Totally give your hurt to God. Only then can he begin the healing of the past. Only then can you be totally free from the memories and pain that keep you in bondage. Only then can you respond to people instead of reacting to them. Only then can you be the victorious Christian God wants you to be instead of the victim.

It's time to talk honestly with God in prayer about how you are feeling. Confess your feelings to him. Give him your resentments, hatred, and bitterness. Ask him to remodel the inside of your head, making it a suitable home for his thoughts.

Some of us have a tendency to gloss over the sins that we need to present to the Lord in confession. Only the "biggie" sins make it out of our mouths before the Lord. You have your own idea of what the "biggies" are, but I perceive them as murder, adultery, homosexuality. Only rarely do I confess gossiping, backbiting, and envy. God does not, however, grade sins. They are all the same in his sight.

For example, when pride rears its ugly head, it causes us to be indefinite and vague about what is on our hearts. We may say "Forgive me," when we haven't named the feeling for what it is—sin. Or we may say "I'm sorry," while deep in our hearts what we are sorry about is that we got caught.

"If we confess our *sins* [emphasis mine], he is faithful and just and will forgive us our sins and purify us from all unrighteousness" (1 John 1:9).

On the other hand: "If we claim we have not sinned, we make him out to be a liar and his word has no place in our lives" (1 John 1:10).

Following are stories of two people. Their sins are the same. Their conditions before the Lord are quite different.

"A man whose young, attractive wife was killed by a drunken motorist was left to face the world alone with twins. When the shock had passed, and the edge had come off his grief, he burned with a concentrated hate against his wife's 'murderer.' As a result of his resentments, his home became a bad place in which to live. His children felt they had not only lost a mother to death, but a father to hate."[3]

One resentful woman I counseled prayed about her anger at a co-worker, but confessed nothing to God in the vague statements of her prayer.

"May I suggest that you name what it is you're trying to confess," I said.

She tried again and gave God her frustration and hurt and the feeling of guilt that she had about the anger and resentment. But she did not give God her resentment, did not confess it as sin.

On the third try she was annoyed with me. But again she prayed, this time making her prayer specific and final.

The relief exhibited on her face was confirmation that she had been released. She was set free!

Ask God to show you in Scripture those words that will minister to your need today. Ask him to bring a mature Christian into your life to help you with those things you still have questions about. Seek help from your pastor.

When you have received help with your past hurts, then and only then will you be ready to consider a long-term relationship with another adult.

Are You Remarrying for the Right Reasons?

"Marriage isn't meant to be the solution to personal insecurities," write Bud and Kathy Pearson. "Often when couples remarry, they simply shift all their hang-ups—compounded by the pain, bitterness, and trauma of divorce or bereavement—to the new marriage. It's not surprising that the marriage isn't what it should be. It's not surprising when it fails."[4]

People hurry into remarriage for any number of impractical reasons, such as that it was the only day the pastor had available; all of the kids were home for Christmas; she found a dress on sale but it had long sleeves so it had to be a winter wedding. Do you have an impractical reason of your own?

There are serious reasons, too, that cause rushed nuptials. Identifying them in yourself requires personal integrity followed by a desire to do some painful digging. Following are some of the "real" reasons you may rush into marriage for you to take a look at, talk to God about, and perhaps receive some counsel for before you draw another person into your life, or before you are drawn into someone else's.

1. You are a relationship addict. You are addicted to relationships. You think you need a man or woman to be complete. Your worth is based in having a member of the opposite sex on your arm, or in being that show piece. In other words, you don't have a identity that is your own.

Relationship addiction is the topic of conversation in all kinds of places, from meetings of Adult Children of Alcoholics to Sunday school classes. Robin Norwood, author of the best-selling book *Women Who Love Too Much*, describes relationship addiction as using a man as the drug of choice. Of course, there are men who are relationship addicts, too.

> A woman who uses her relationships as a drug will have fully as much denial about that fact as any chemically addictive individual, and fully as much resistance and fear concerning letting go of her obsessive thinking and highly emotionally charged way of interacting with men. But usually, if she is gently but firmly confronted, she will at some level recognize the power of her relationship addiction and know that she is in the grip of a pattern over which she has lost control.[5]

Taking extra time is critical, in your case, to allow the wound to heal from the previous death or divorce. You need time to realize and accept the truth—another relationship or remarriage is not the answer to your problem. It's like a dog chasing its tail. You end up back where you started. The answer to your problem lies within you, not in another man or woman.

Mary, a never-married recovering alcoholic, gives good advice to the many women she encounters who suffer from relationship addiction. She recommends one whole year without dating. "No men," she says firmly. "You'll discover that you *can* get along."

When you are a complete and healthy person as an individual and really believe you do not need another person to make you whole, then consider remarriage.

2. *You are a helpless person.* You need a mommy/wife or a daddy/husband to take care of you and solve your problems. You feel, act, and sometimes even look like a helpless victim. The first man or woman who comes along who shows you affection will seem like Mr. or Miss "Right." Questions that may be running through your mind are, Why do I need him (her) so badly? Am I being super careful of my words for fear I might offend him (her)? When we have a disagreement, why do I feel like he (she) will leave and never come back? Why can't I make a decision for myself?

For some reason you are consumed with self-doubt. People overwhelm you and you feel inferior. You have allowed others to control your life, believing you need them. In all probability you are an approval seeker, a people pleaser, a "yes man."

"I was such a chameleon," said Joan. "I found my approval in what I thought others wanted me to be." She now knows that obeying God and bringing him glory is enough approval.

Robert Subby, author of *Lost in the Shuffle,* says,

> In this process of relentless approval-seeking, we gradually deny much of who and what we really are. Always alert and focused on others to get our needs met, we never have

time to focus on ourselves in any other than a superficial way. And this has obvious consequences for how we see ourselves, how we view others and how we get along in the world.[6]

You may as well be wearing a sandwich board advertising yourself "Here I am, helpless and inferior," because out there waiting for you is your Nemesis, a person who needs to control you.

And you *will* find one another.

3. *You are a controller.* You receive your worth by taking care of Hilda or Harry Helpless, solving problems that are not yours. You suffer from a distorted notion of power and control. Unknowingly, you look for someone who needs you and you go to work on her. You go to great lengths to teach her and train her, maybe even shower her with gifts. You make decisions for her. Any sign of responsible behavior on her part threatens you. You fear not being needed.

At some point in my life I learned to define "taking care of" (or fixing or controlling) someone else as altogether different from "caring for" someone. "Taking care of" someone takes away that person's responsibility for himself or herself and enables irresponsibility. What is the payoff for taking care of someone else? Are you looking for affirmation? Is it simply the power of having someone under your control? Depending on you?

I'm a reformed controller. When I look back at all the responsibility I took for other people, I wonder how I managed! Controlling is a self-induced form of insanity.

It should be pointed out, however, not all beneficiaries of the controller's attention are irresponsible. One woman's husband controlled her with his anger. She was terrified to make him angry. "Peace at all costs" was her motto. When she began to get emotionally healthy herself, he internalized his anger, making an already diagnosed problem with impotence even more pronounced. So controlling as a way of life can be detrimental to other than the one being controlled.

At the same time, the controlled probably has not gained mastery over his or her own life. Both men and women fall comfortably into this sick relationship pattern. But because "mothering" is born into women, they already have the job mastered. Don't settle for a sick codependent existence when you could have a healthy male/female relationship.

Codependency is itself an addiction to other people, to things, or to a particular behavior. Those trapped in codependent relationships, I believe, instinctively despise them, but they often do not know how to stop themselves. They will express their anger at the lack of appreciation received from the one they are controlling. They will say, "I'll quit doing things for her and see if she even notices." Beware! The slippery slide to martyrdom starts here.

The simple truth is no one wants to be emotionally handicapped, let alone have someone make them that way. That is what we do when we make decisions and choices for others; we treat them as though they are incapable of caring for and deciding for themselves.

4. *You are a leech.* You are not a giver. You are a taker. "The leech has two daughters. 'Give! Give!' they cry" (Prov. 30:15).

God has created us so we can both give and receive strength. There are times when we all need to lean on someone else. But the leech only drains energy, time, friendship.

Often leeches do not like their own behavior. They may even know why. But do they take authority over their own lives and get some help for those things that keep them in bondage? Probably not. They are more likely to find someone of the opposite sex and leech the person till he or she is empty. Those so dissatisfied with themselves or their situation can discover in such a sick relationship the most encompassing substitute for self-contentment. Ironically, they can also muster the effort required to maintain it.

One woman, twice married and twice divorced, dated a man with a long-term proclivity for alcohol. He knew he had it. She knew he had it. But somehow he convinced her to bear his burden for him. She was a Christian who wanted to serve. He took advantage of her Christian charity. He even made a show of accepting Christ as his Savior. But he did not change his lifestyle. He leeched her dry.

There are times when we need to be forthright and say no to those who would use us. At the same time, those who are easily misled or caught up in this kind of trap need to learn from their mistakes. They are a combination of a relationship addict and the person who gains worth being a caretaker.

Conclusion

It is easy to see that there are personality and behavior problems which, in the case of the blame games, essentially involve only the person doing the blaming. The choice is yours. You can take the responsibility for your own behavior. It is liberating to grow up and be willing to accept the consequences for the choices you make.

When you are considering remarriage, taking a double look—at yourself and at the potential mate—is necessary. Seeking to recognize whether or not you fall into one of the other categories we have considered will take some honest searching. Are you a relationship addict? Is that why you are pushing for remarriage? Do you like to control someone else? Is the person you've chosen for remarriage "helpless"? Are you a leech? Or are you being leeched? Don't gloss over this section. Take time to answer truthfully. Perhaps you need to do some more reading on the subject or exploratory talking with a counselor or close friend. (See "Suggestions for Further Reading.")

4

An Ounce of Prevention Is Still Worth a Pound of Cure

May 1980, Lake Miltona, Minnesota.

Six of us gathered to open the walleye fishing season—for me an introduction to extended family as well as to the rigors of compulsive fishing.

After day one I thought I might "sleep in" the next morning, lie in the sun, and read a book. But in the early morning hours of day two I thought, "But what if the fish are really biting this morning? I don't want to miss it!"

I was hooked, almost as securely as the man who was courting me. I was, I believe, on trial to see if I could be a suitable wife for a fisherman/hunter. Bud proposed to me during that fishing trip. Apparently I had passed muster.

And so had he. But I knew that if I couldn't tolerate the hobbies of an avid outdoorsman, I would make him a miserable wife. In accepting his love of the outdoors, my own interests were broadened and deepened.

51

Even our eight-day honeymoon was spent in the backwoods of Ontario, Canada. We fished every day, eight or more hours each day.

"I don't know whether this marriage is going to work or not," Bud told my children on our return. "After the fifth day of fishing eight to ten hours a day, your mother began to whine about wanting to go to shore."

Primary Relationship Issues

Do you need to make a decision about whether or not you are compatible with the person you are seeing? Let's talk about the issues you, individually and as a couple, will be facing as you contemplate remarriage—things you should think about, talk about, and perhaps come to conclusions about before you set a date for your wedding. No one else needs to be involved in these discussions or decisions.

We are not talking about what color the bride should wear or whether or not the groom should give his best man cuff links. We will go into those "small" decisions in another chapter. Here the issues are bigger—those things that need to be discussed while you are still deciding whether remarriage is for you.

Neither will we deal with other relationships right now. There will be plenty of opportunities after remarriage to become involved with the children from one or both of your previous marriages, your brothers and sisters, your parents and in-laws, your previous in-laws, and the outlaws.

Sexuality

Does God relax his commandments on sexual sin for those over forty, or for those who have been married before?

No, sexual immorality is no less a sin in God's eyes because we are older or because our status in life has changed. He is not interested in net worth or background. Today we continue to hear a lot of credence given to sexuality by the secular world. "What 'responsible adults' or 'consenting adults' do behind closed doors," they say, "is no one else's business." As if God cannot see you behind a closed door. It doesn't cut ice with God. Fornication is still fornication and still a grievous sin in God's eyes.

"I believe God has brought us together because we need each other," I said to Marni, a chaplain at a Minneapolis hospital. We were discussing my living arrangements before I became a Christian, before Bud came into my life. "I can't believe God would want us to split up," I continued.

"That all may be true," Marni replied, "but God still does not approve of fornication."

I was jarred by the word, thrown back in my chair.

"What a nasty word!" I thought. It was startling to be thought of as a fornicator, and worse yet to acknowledge it of myself. Why was it wrong for me? Society had decided during the sexual revolution of the sixties and seventies that sex outside of marriage was okay. I had simply bought into that philosophy.

Marni assured me God had not changed his mind.

You may not be familiar with the word *fornication*. It is not a word that gets used very often these days. What does it mean? It simply means sexual immorality—premarital or extramarital sex or any sexual intercourse that takes place outside the bounds of holy matrimony.

How is it used in the Bible? Listen to God's Word on the subject. "You shall not commit adultery" is the seventh of the Ten Commandments. These were not "suggestions" written on disposable tablets, but absolute commandments carved in stone. When we say, "This decision isn't carved in stone, we can still change it," it explains how long lasting God's commandments are.

"Flee from sexual immorality. All other sins a man commits are outside his body, but he who sins sexually sins against his own body. Do you not know that your body is a temple of the Holy Spirit, who is in you, whom you have received from God? You are not your own; you were bought at a price. Therefore honor God with your body" (1 Cor. 6:18–20).

"But among you there must not be even a hint of sexual immorality, or of any kind of impurity, or of greed, because these are improper for God's holy people" (Eph. 5:3).

"It is God's will that you should be holy; that you should avoid sexual immorality" (1 Thess. 4:3).

One woman explained that after her husband died she did not know what to do with her sexual yearnings. She envisioned a silver platter where she placed all of her feelings of loss and hunger for touching. She then offered it to the Lord, saying, "Here, I don't know what to do with these feelings. You take them." She said that while she still had the longings, she knew that God could be trusted to guide her and fulfill her needs.

Another woman used the words *skin hungry* to describe her feelings of needing to be touched. She has learned to be forthright and ask her friends for a hug when she needs one. She is also quick to give others much-needed hugs.

One thing is sure: You will need to set sexual boundaries in your relationship if you haven't already. Decide together where you will draw the line on sexual matters. Purpose together to keep your relationship pure before you marry. The absence of guilt and sorrow will be the best wedding gift you could give each other.

A recent study of 4,000 Swedish women showed that those who lived with their husbands before marriage were 80 percent more likely to separate or divorce than women who did not. Women who spent more than three years living with their future husbands were especially likely to divorce or separate.[1]

"We are not saying that living together actually causes divorce," Yale University sociologist Neil Bennett says. "What we are saying is that it appears that couples who live together premaritally are less committed to the values and interests typically associated with marriage and are more inclined to accept divorce."[2]

"Middle-aged men and women 'dating' and having sexual alliances . . . if not downright immoral, were regarded as unnatural and unseemly at their age," said secular writers Bernice and Morton Hunt, referring to attitudes that were holdovers from earlier in the century. "But," they continue, "as national attitudes toward middle age have changed and sexual activity in married middle-aged people has come to seem natural and proper, it has come to seem equally so in postmarital middle-aged people."[3]

The authors' "enlightened" opinion was characteristic of the midseventies. While they discredited those who believed that sex outside of marriage was wrong, they believed, as many did then and still do, that lifestyles and sexual preferences are individual rights and no one else's business.

It should not surprise Christians to see statistics and attitudes like the above. The world is "still doing it." But living together before marriage is nevertheless not part of God's plan for our lives.

I hope it goes without saying that Christians should not participate in trial marriage. Living together before the wedding ceremony is a flagrant sin in God's eyes.

What About Children in Middle Age?

While we are on the topic of sex, it seems important to mention children—more specifically, pregnancy.

Do I hear snorts and screams of laughter? Remember Sarah, Abraham's wife? That's how she responded when God sent his messengers by Abraham's tent one hot day to say, "I will surely return to you about this time next year, and Sarah your wife will have a son" (Gen. 18:10a). Listening at the entrance of the tent, verse 12 tells us, "Sarah laughed to herself as she thought, 'After I am worn out and my master is old, will I now have this pleasure?'"

I am not suggesting that God will intervene so you could miraculously conceive and bear a child in your old age (although I sincerely believe he could). The point I want to make is that people over forty *do* bear children.

Childbearing years for women extend into the middle forties to early fifties on an average. Men, seemingly, are able to father children much longer.

This is an area of discussion that should not be left to

guesswork or chance. For a forty-five-year-old woman to turn up pregnant can be a traumatic experience. For her husband it can be equally troublesome.

One woman related that after only a few months of marriage in her middle age she discovered she was pregnant. When she told her husband, he became very angry, blamed her totally for the predicament, and said, "I don't want children. I already have grown children." And he left her.

Don't leave childbearing or pregnancy to chance. Careless optimism has created more than one unplanned change-of-life baby.

Where Will You Live?

Many couples marry and move into the home where one of them has been living. Sometimes it works.

For Bud and me it has worked. But there were several years when I wondered if we might have made a mistake. We had not really talked about this aspect of our marriage. We had only decided where we would live in terms of the city. Would he move to Minneapolis where I lived? Or would I move to Cedar Rapids where he lived? I believed keeping my job and asking him to move into my territory would not be the right foot on which to begin a marriage. It was assumed I would move into his house in Cedar Rapids. To that end he began construction plans for enlarging his house to accommodate me and my daughter.

He assumed. And I assumed.

While I am thankful it was not the home where he had lived with his first wife and family, there was still tension simply because it was his home and not our home. I felt constrained in the first two or three years to be careful about changing too many things, about taking away the masculine appearance, adding a feminine touch.

Now, after nearly ten years, the home is ours and is a beautiful example of both of our tastes. I shall never forget, though, Bud's astounded expression on the first Christmas when I tied the red-and-white polka dot bow on the mounted speckled belly goose hanging over the Franklin stove.

There are other more traumatic examples of combining households. Moving to a home where the previous spouse's tastes in decorating and style remain is difficult, especially for women. Ghosts linger in bedrooms where the previous marriage may have been consummated, or where children were conceived.

"New house, new start" is a good principle if economically possible. Starting fresh in a neutral place is recommended. Some counselors even suggest that a remarrying older couple establish their new home at a distance from both of their families if they are to escape the pressures placed on them by other family members.

What Are Your Expectations of Each Other?

Usually men and women marrying after forty do so knowing who they are and where they are going. Gone are the days of uncertainty. Both people are more mature, experienced. Careers are established or retirement is around the corner. What each person will get from the marriage would seem to be more easily defined. But is it?

By the time a couple is acquainted for a length of time (it will vary with each couple because of personalities), they should be familiar with one another's bents—the habits and behaviors that make them unique individuals. Still, some couples willfully (or wishfully) ignore traits that lead to unnecessary conflict and, sometimes, open warfare.

Once in our second or third year of marriage at a couples' group meeting we were doing an exercise designed to promote communication. We were asked to list ten things we liked to do most. The idea was to list "together" kinds of things, then talk about them.

My husband, the rascal, listed his ten favorite things as follows:

1. Duck hunting
2. Turkey hunting

3. Goose hunting
4. Pheasant hunting
5. Quail hunting
6. Walleye fishing
7. Crappie fishing
8. Bluegill fishing
9. Trout fishing
10. Fishing with my wife

He received lots of laughs from the group. While it was undoubtedly Bud's defense against his discomfort in sharing personal things in group situations, I accepted it as a joke, realizing at the same time there was a grain of truth in his list.

What kinds of things have you done while dating? Do you enjoy the same things?

Unwise men and women expect their mates to give up those things that bring them individual pleasure, opting instead for being together as a couple all of the time. I try to imagine the shell of a person I would have received at remarriage had I taken that approach. He would not have been the man I was attracted to.

Talking about these things before marriage is important. Reaching an understanding or agreement through compromise on those hours to be spent individually and also determining to spend time together on specific hobbies or activities should be a priority.

No one, man or woman, entering into a marriage should expect to have all of the hours of freedom that are available to singles.

Bud does not spend as much time hunting and fishing as he did before we were married. His sports had filled much of the lonely time in his life. Anyway, I like to fish, too, so now he can have the best of both worlds—fishing and having his beloved in the boat with him.

I have always wondered what couples who spend every minute of every day together talk about. If neither of them does anything alone, what is there to tell a spouse? They each know what the other has done because both have been there. Dreary!

One attribute of maturity is to be able to handle the conflict between wanting to be connected to another and the need for separateness. If a person is so uncomfortable with being alone that he or she experiences anxiety, perhaps relationship addiction is a problem. Are you dependent on someone else? Do you feel safe and reassured only if you are with someone? You may be relying on another person rather than God to fulfill your relationship needs. I can think of three reasons not to. First, we set ourselves up to be disappointed and rejected. Second, we put an incredible responsibility on a friend or lover. Third, perhaps most important, we deny ourselves the chance to see how completely God can and will fill all of our relationship needs.

Many times I have chosen to talk by phone to a friend or have asked my husband for his ear to work out a perceived problem or need. At that point I felt I needed someone with skin on. That's okay, but I have also found that when I need someone, I can go to God first, pray, take time to read Scripture, jot notes in my journal and then wait for God to answer. It is so wonderful when I sense his presence. There are many verses that I could give you that have helped me, but most often the psalms are a comfort when I feel lonely or alone.

Having time alone is important. I want my husband to have hobbies and interests that are his alone. And I want to have my own, too. I want to remain mysterious to my husband. I do not expect him to entertain me. I can thank God for that, because even if I did expect him to, he wouldn't.

One woman, whose second divorce occurred because of her husband's possessiveness, said, "I never had time to myself, even to pluck my eyebrows in the bathroom. If I were to do it again, I would have my own leisure guaranteed in a written agreement."[4]

Beth, a widow of several years, told how she had hoped something good might come of her friendship with a man a few years younger than herself. One day she prayed, "Lord, let me see him exactly as he is."

"When he left my home that evening, I said to myself, 'He's boring.'" Beth had thought it through and realized she would not want to spend her remaining years with someone whose company bored her.

"For their part, few men at this time of life want to be the total support for a clinging vine. 'I found after I married Clara, that she couldn't even balance her checkbook. The dependency that seemed kind of appealing when we were going together became oppressive after we were married, and I had to help her decide everything,' confessed an insurance salesman."[5]

We honor each other by allowing space. I, for example, enjoy symphony music. Bud does not. He encouraged me to buy myself a season ticket. In conversation with Ed, a friend in his nineties, Bud learned that he also enjoyed the symphony. He suggested Ed and I go together. So each month I would drive by for Ed, and together we enjoyed an evening of symphony music. I might have been reluctant to go by myself, so this was a perfect solution.

Discussion Starters

There are fat and thin people, mean and gentle people, bald and hairy people, rich and poor people. There are different tastes in furniture—modern or antique. We make choices in food and drink. If we are astute we can identify overindulgence in those areas, too.

Are you outgoing and your friend introverted? Will that change after marriage? Are you justifying his lack of interest in your friends by saying to yourself, maybe to others, "He'll be more comfortable after he knows them better?" Can you accept her extroverted personality? Or do you want her to change? Would you like him better if he were more subdued?

If you answer yes more than once to the above questions, you had better rethink your choice of mate. Or you had better examine your expectations. You are headed for disappointment.

Is the person you care for a night person or a day person? Some couples have conflicts about bedtime. When one person in the marriage likes to stay up till the wee hours, the other person can begin to feel rejected and unloved when he or she goes to bed alone each night. Hasn't everyone thought at one time or another, "I wonder if my mate doesn't care for me anymore?" Early discussion and compromise on these areas that involve both of you will see you over some bumps in the matrimonial road ahead.

Are you sloppy or neat? Discuss who will be expected to pick up after you if you are a slob. Are you counting on your new wife or husband to do it? You had better let him or her in on the secret. As you spend time at one another's homes, look at the order (or lack of it) in the home. That's probably what you are going to get when you're married.

When I first met Bud, his dining room table was piled with mail and other papers. After ten years of marriage, I am still the one who throws old papers, magazines, invoices, and letters away. And the minute I do so, Bud says, "Have you seen that letter from so-and-so?" I have realized that it would not matter if the letter were fifty years old. The day I toss it is the day he will miss it.

Do you like sports and she opera? Are you an outdoor nut and your partner a couch potato?

One couple had trouble with leisure-time activities. The woman still had young people from her previous marriage involved in sports, both in high school and college. She wanted to attend their football games and other athletic events. Her husband wanted her to be with him on their boat. She was willing to compromise and occasionally miss one of her sons' games. Her husband was never willing to compromise. Instant conflict!

Too many times in my own marriage I have experienced needless disappointments because I did not say what my expectations were. I have also experienced unnecessary anxiety because I have not checked out my husband's expectations of me. Sometimes the things we expect are unrealistic.

It's time in your thinking about marriage to sit down together and talk through some of these questions. Many of the areas for discussion seem, on the surface, to be simplistic things. It is surprising, however, to know how many of these "little," unimportant things become major problems over time. Find out now how well you know this person to whom you are thinking of making a marriage commitment.

Our pastor on the occasion of his and his wife's thirtieth wedding anniversary said, "The most important decision I made in my life was to accept Jesus as my Lord and Savior. The second most important decision was when I married Mary Lou."

Not only is it an important decision, but the transition from the single to the married state is one of the most difficult and challenging decisions you will ever make. Careful and thorough preparation is highly important. Unfortunately, many couples do spend more time planning the wedding—clothing, flowers, guest lists, music—than they do in preparation for their lives together. The results are too often disastrous!

Talk about your hobbies and leisure-time activities. Are either of you currently doing things with the other you really don't enjoy? If you are, will you keep doing it after you marry? Do you resent having to go shopping at the mall with her every weekend? Are you feeling like a martyr every time you go to the sporting goods store with him?

One woman described her horror to discover that her new husband read pornographic magazines. It was never revealed in their discussions prior to marriage. After the marriage there were a few tense moments as she confronted him with her knowledge, related the hurt she felt, and asked him to stop looking at and reading them.

What kinds of things did each of you do before meeting? Talk about those things you enjoy individually. See if your friend may enjoy them. If not, talk about whether or not you will want to find another friend with whom you can play bridge or golf.

Would you ask your new mate to give up a hobby he enjoys? Suppose your intended bride sewed and had the dining room table cluttered with fabric and sewing notions all the time. Could you accept that? Would you be willing to give up your hobby? Think about it.

Talk about vacations. Where have you each vacationed in previous years? Describe your most memorable vacation and why you enjoyed it. Tell each other what you really consider a good vacation. See how you will enjoy spending vacation time together.

Some couples have times when they vacation separately from their mates. Men go on fishing or hunting trips. Women go to the city to shop and spend a few days going to plays and museums.

Bud and I find that enjoyable. Of course, we always have vacation times together, too. But I love Florida and he doesn't. My theory is that if I persuaded him to go with me, he really would not enjoy it. Then I would be so concerned for him that my own pleasure in the ocean, sand, and sun would be diminished. On the other hand, because I enjoy fishing so much, the only time I would not want to go with him is when he goes moose hunting in Saskatchewan. Nothing against the Canadian province. Moose hunting just doesn't appeal to me.

How do you handle day-to-day communications? Are you both able to talk and share your feelings? Does one of you do most of the talking about the day's events, or are both of you verbal and able to communicate openly? If communication is not open and easy while you are courting, the chances of it changing to complete openness after you walk down the aisle are somewhere between slim and none.

My husband does not bubble over with enthusiasm the minute he walks into the house at night. Neither is he ready to listen to me effervesce about my day. That was a conflict until we talked it through.

Talk about food. What is your favorite restaurant and why? Do you favor Chinese and he hates it? Or Mexican and she gets sick from it? What kind of a cook are you? Maybe the male in your partnership is the chef. Will you feel pushed out of "your" kitchen if he is? Or will that make you happy? Does she prepare heavy, calorie-laden food and you prefer low calorie fresh vegetables and fruits?

What about entertaining? Before our marriage, I think, Bud might have had the men who fished with him (and maybe their wives) over for a fish fry once every year or so. I thoroughly enjoy entertaining and would probably have our home open every weekend. My husband needs a little more solitude, though, so I have learned to be more moderate. Will you agree on entertaining in your home? Will you agree on going to others' homes?

Do you have friends in common? Or will you both be making new friends, perhaps in a new place? It is not easy to find friends where both the men and women are compatible. Often, if he likes and enjoys spending time with one of the men he works with, you might not enjoy the guy's wife. Trust God to bring people into your life to become the close friends every couple desires. Ask him to help you still be available as Christ's ambassador in those other relationships.

Handling Differences

What if you don't agree on everything? (Get serious! You don't really think you *do* agree on everything, do you?) How are you going to handle those differences? Can you accept a mate who watches television more than you care to? What will you do when the television becomes a big issue?

"Steve was a football nut," said Jan. "I watched a couple of games with him but made it known there would be a limit to how much I would watch. We hardly ever watch TV now. Other things have become priorities to us."

These are issues that need to be discussed and resolved

before marriage, not after. Are you willing to fight and fight fair until there is a resolution?

Helene, a German woman who met and married a German man through an ad in a Hamburg magazine, said, "Even though it was our first marriage, I said unless he agreed that we sit down when there was a problem and discuss it all the way through, no way would I marry him."

She and Walter have done this, perhaps still with her insisting, and the air is clear. There is no hidden agenda in their marriage.

Have you expressed anger or disappointment to this person with whom you are thinking about spending the remainder of your life? It is not reasonable to expect that you will never be angry or disappointed. How will you handle disharmony?

One woman explained that when she and her husband disagree about something and she tells him, he hears an altogether different message. When she says, "Honey, I disagree with you," he hears "Honey, you are wrong; therefore, you are no good." Do you hear things that are not being said? Do you assume you know what is meant without checking it out? How would you resolve this kind of misunderstanding?

I thank God he changes us—if we allow him to. Before Christ came into my life, I loved to argue. I could make an argument out of almost anything. I argued until the opposition gave up. Until, that is, our family received therapy and we learned how to fight fair. I'll never forget it. We had learned to communicate feelings and had practiced it with our counselors. One night I tried it out on a member of my family.

"I'm angry because you didn't come home and help with the picnic preparation," I said. "I feel like I do everything and I'm taken for granted."

I didn't say "you always" and "you never."

"I'm sorry you feel that way," he responded. "I feel like you have expectations without telling me what they are."

After repeating my unhappiness with the situation, he

said, "What do you want me to do about it?" In playing fair
rather than attacking the other person there was nothing
left to be said. I was angry. He was sorry I felt that way but
pointed out that while I had expectations, I hadn't communicated them to him. The argument ended right there. And
I learned that I would have to do something else with the
anger I felt. He was not willing that I dump it on him. What
do you do with your anger? Do you bottle it, or does it
burst from you?

What is the other person's spirit like? Is there joy or
depression?

Bud once said he felt a spirit of joy in our home in
Minnesota. He liked it. That should have been a clue for me
that joy did not reside in his home. Later I would struggle
with how to handle his contemplative moods. Bud took
longer to make decisions than I. I had interpreted his pon-
dering as a mood. Bud reminds me that men are often ana-
lytical while women are more emotional.

One woman described how her husband holds onto hurt
longer than she does. While he's working through it he is
unapproachable. She had to learn to leave him alone.

In the beginning of our marriage I took the moods very
personally. If I did not ask aloud, I always wondered, "What
did I do?" But with time and conversation (after the fact) I
discovered that 99 percent of the time I was not part of the
problem or its resolution.

A sentence that has carried me through many a painful
trial is, *It's not about me.* Over and over again I have had to
let go of how I'm feeling and trust God with the outcome
of situations. Sometimes I have had to say to Bud, "I don't
think it's about me. If it is, you need to tell me. Meanwhile,
I'm here. I love you and I'm ready to listen when or if you
want to talk."

It's not about me gives me the freedom from taking
responsibility for how someone else is feeling. Most other
people also have problems, and many times the rejection I
think I am feeling really is a problem inside them.
Something is going on in the other persons' life that does

not involve me. It's true that if we knew how little others think of us, we would not spend so much time or energy worrying about that matter.

The trick in assessing values is to come to an agreement on the really important things. Recognize that you will disagree on some things, and decide in advance how you will handle them.

You cannot change the other person. Success or failure in a relationship is not determined by how well we can get others to do what we think they ought to do. What should you do? Retreat behind resentment? Nurse a grudge?

Neither is acceptable. Your responsibility is to answer the question, How can I love and accept this person and help him or her aim for the best? Then the focus is on you, not on the other person.

My daughter Sara, who was in her early teens at the time, and I went for some mother/daughter counseling. The counselor had us do a short multiple choice quiz with no right or wrong answers. One of the questions was, "If you had a free day to do whatever you choose, would you a) read a book, b) take a walk in the woods, c) spend time with friends, d) go shopping?"

My daughter and I consistently chose different answers for all ten questions. Did I love her less? Of course not. But it revealed how important it is not to assume that we all like the same things. The same would seem to be true with married people.

"Celebrate the differences," the counselor said. He meant, I think, that we should enjoy the variety of people within our own families, accept their differences, and learn from them.

I have listened to men and women in marriages where there is no acceptance of the different likes and dislikes. The message is, "If you like something and I don't, you're wrong." Someone who fusses and constantly gives a mate problems for doing what he or she enjoys is stealing joy while at the same time attempting to control the mate. It takes a strong and self-confident person to withstand someone's constant anger or negative attitude. Would it really make you happy if the person you loved was exactly like you? I think that would be terribly boring and unfulfilling.

Don't Look Back

It is said that "a bird in the hand is worth two in the bush." But when current problems become unpleasant, some men and women are tempted to look back in the bushes and recall the past. Unfortunately our memories are selective and perhaps not as clear as they may be. When there are troubles today, we tend to look at our past in a different, more flattering light.

I call that kind of thinking "longing for the leeks and onions of Egypt." Comparing and saying "At least I never had this problem with so-and-so" gets you nowhere. In fact, it creates more dissatisfaction and unhappiness.

"If I had it to do over, I would learn more about the marriage I was getting into before I allowed myself to get into it," said Elaine. Well, she can't start over, but she can begin to do what is right today.

Some couples may need pre-remarriage counseling. A counselor may be able to help those considering joining together in holy rematrimony see more clearly what challenges they will encounter. An unbiased third party may be able to see similarities in the present relationship and the previous marriage and bring them to the attention of the counselees.

While starry-eyed lovers have their place in fiction, in real-life drama it is the persons with their eyes wide open and clearly focused who have a better chance of living happily ever after.

The couple's relationship must be the primary relationship, the foundation for the remarriage. If a house has a firm foundation, then building, maintenance, and repair are worthwhile and can be done. But if the foundation is shaky or crumbling, piling on additional stresses from other family members will only weaken it more. Day-to-day irritations are like rain leaking through the ground and into the basement. Do not take the foundational relationship for granted. It needs constant nurture.

How did you come out? Have you decided you've chosen the perfect woman or man with whom to spend the rest of your life? Is this the person whom God has brought into your life to be your mate? Or did you learn through your discussions that there are too many conflicts and differences? Would your remarriage be a failure?

There will still be questions. There will still be problems. No marriage relationship is completely trouble free.

Bud and I still have questions—some verbalized, some only thought about in the darkness of our minds. Did we wait long enough before remarrying? Could we have been better prepared? There were things we should have discussed and resolved before we took our vows. We are also both totally aware that looking back serves no purpose.

Our marriage has not been, and is not today, perfect. If there is a perfect marriage, I don't know about it. However, in spite of the problems and the hurts that are typical of the first years of any marriage, Bud and I were then, as we are now, ten years later, committed to each other until death parts us. We love one another as much as is humanly possible and as much as each of us allows Christ to love through us.

5

Marrying the Multitudes: Secondary Relationships

A couple of years into Bud's and my marriage we were visiting his father in Little Rock. Mealtimes were usually times of reminiscing. Interesting facts, as well as perceived feelings about the family, came out. I had not been in the family long enough to contribute, so I listened carefully, watching facial expressions and body language.

I no longer remember who broached the subject, but a disagreement ensued about the year Bud's mother had died.

"Dad, it was in 1957," said Bud. "I was stationed in Georgia, and you got me moved to Fort Leonard Wood, Missouri."

Mr. Hunter remembered "helping" Bud get his orders changed so that he could be nearer to home during his mother's last illness. Bud, on the other hand, remembered that he had had no say in the matter. Even though he was in his midtwenties, his father had made the decision without consulting him and had persevered in getting the Army to change his base location.

Now twenty-five years later they were talking about it for the first time. As an observer I could see on Bud's father's face the pain of discovery of a wrong done. And I could see the root of bitterness disengaged from a grown son's heart as feelings and memories were exchanged.

Family of Origin

The family in which you were raised affects you for the rest of your life.

"Our present lives are attached to our previous families as if by an umbilical cord," writes David Field, marriage and family therapist. "Our behavior and thoughts, our attitudes and reactions, and our values and beliefs are all linked to the family from which we came."[1]

Your family of origin is the place where you spent most time as a child. For many people it was in a home with a mom and a dad. Were you an only child or did you have siblings? Stepmothers or stepfathers played roles in some of our lives. Others may have been raised in a foster home or by an adoptive family.

"We cannot escape our past when we move into marriage," says Field. "Our experiences affect how we view all of life—career, family relationships, and our own attitude toward God."[2]

Couples who remarry in midlife or older may or may not still have living parents or siblings. But they will undoubtedly have a string of other secondary relationships to deal with. Unlike young couples who marry, from the very beginning older couples have much larger, built-in, extended families.

But for now, let's consider a look at the family or the home you came from. What character traits have you brought with you from your family? What personality strengths and weaknesses do you have that have come from your family of origin?

When my son, Stephen, was in his late twenties he took his grandmother and her husband (my stepfather) on a trip to Washington State to visit my mother's side of the family. Steve had previously met only a couple of his great-aunts when they visited our home in Minnesota.

We laugh now as he tells how excited they all were to get together for a family picnic. Expecting a rousing and noisy time with such a large family, Steve was surprised at how they all just sat quietly—no one saying anything for long stretches of time—each in their own private reverie. After fifteen or twenty minutes, one of them might make a comment or ask a question which would bring a brief response, a smile, a laugh, but seldom animated conversation. Steve was accustomed to lots of conversation within our home when he was growing up and from his paternal relatives. Will our family picnics be like this as we all age?

Why are some children different from, and some carbon copies of their parents? Each of us comes "prepackaged" with a distinctive personality with both strengths and weaknesses, some of which are learned from our parents. With all of that raw material in place, we must choose what we do with it. With spirits surrendered to God and sincere desire to be who he wants us to be, weaknesses can be turned into strengths.

As I look back at my family of origin I see a dysfunctional home—communication-wise. There just was not much deep communication. My parents' reticence in communicating undoubtedly was handed down from their own families of origin.

Recently Bud and I vacationed with two other couples, all of us over fifty, and without exception each of us described our parents' inability to communicate with us as children, particularly about death, illness, tragedy, or problems within the family. That is not to say they were bad parents. Communicating, telling everything, apparently did not have the emphasis then that it has today.

Today my mother, bless her heart, still finds it difficult to say how she is feeling. She tries valiantly to hide her feelings of sorrow, grief, or fear behind her stoic German upbringing: chin up, bite back those tears.

I could deal with my feelings in the same way, I suppose. Fortunately, I have been privileged to grow older in a world proliferating with good advice—from books by men and women with the same values as mine to the Bible, the most important book from which to gather information—on how to respond to and relate to others. I have chosen to be up front with my thoughts and feelings.

On a recent trip to South Carolina I was along for the ride, so to speak. While Bud attended a week-long school, I journeyed around Spartanburg and Greenville, made a day trip to Charlotte, North Carolina, and generally got acquainted with the area. But in the evenings, I looked forward to some conversation with my husband. He was understandably preoccupied with studying for his next day's class.

"I'm really lonesome," I said one evening. "I've been alone for three days. I miss people." I had said how I was feeling. I hoped, I suppose, that he would give me a few minutes of his time. I didn't think I was putting pressure on him.

But that is apparently what Bud felt, and he responded, "I knew I shouldn't have brought you along." He threw the responsibility for my loneliness squarely back on me. One word led to another, and I finally went to bed, still lonely; Bud stayed up late studying, still angry.

The next morning though, after time to think about it, Bud greeted me with a good morning hug and an apology.

"I learned my communication skills from my dad," he said. "I hope you understand." There it was—family of origin behavior again.

I did understand. But I didn't excuse it. It is never too late to learn different behavior. Each of us has the power to decide what we will say, how we will respond to our mates or anyone else. We can choose to speak or respond in old destructive ways or we can choose to respond in love.

Studies over the past few years have revealed much about learned behaviors. It is no secret that children who were abused in their families of origin often turn out to be child abusers in their own families. Young men who watched or were aware that their fathers beat their mothers regularly, are often wife beaters today. Women who grew up in homes with alcoholic parents often either become problem drinkers like their mothers, or marry men who are problem drinkers like their fathers.

What is going on in your family of origin? Take a good look at your parents. What has been their pattern? Their personality? Is your family riddled with chemical dependency? Can you see a pattern of alcohol abuse for more than one generation? Beware; this may be your leaning, too. Or you may be attracted to your prospective spouse because he or she is just like your mother or father, one of whom may have been an alcohol abuser. We choose mates who are very often like our parents.

One golden-aged woman has been remarried for over twenty-five years. The man was fun loving and gentle when she married him, but over the years he has become more rigid and more angry. When he is together with his living siblings, they all comment, "He's just like our dad was—a cantankerous old geezer."

Is there a history of abuse in your family of origin? How about you—man or woman—are you a beater? Or are either of you victims of abuse? These behaviors usually do not stop without help, preferably from God, but perhaps also through counseling.

Are your parents stingy or are they spendthrifts? Whatever their behavior and lifestyle, you have undoubtedly learned from them. And if you are not already exhibiting some of the same characteristics, you may still. Today is the day to begin to do what is right. And the plumb line for right living (righteousness) is the Word of God. "The entrance of your words gives light; it gives understanding to the simple" (Ps. 119:130).

How about the family of this man or woman you are either already married to or are thinking of remarrying? Look at them, too. You can glean valuable information by watching, listening, and carefully asking questions both of your mate and his or her family of origin. What are his or her parents like? How do they relate to one another? Is there a loving and communicative relationship between them, or is there strife and unhappiness? Whatever is there, that is what your new mate will expect and that is probably also what he or she will give.

How does your man treat his mother? That's how you will be treated. How does your woman respond to her father? Has all of the "old business" been resolved? Is she hostile to him or loving? That's how you will be treated.

Many families of origin have healthy relationships. Joanne commented that when she met Jim's mother she felt as though she had found her own mom again. "I wish I could have known her mother," said Joanne's husband, Jim. "I think my parents and hers would have gotten along great." Here was a mate's family of origin where comfort and compatibility were felt.

Our parents, whether living or dead, and no matter what our ages, have been our role models. We have learned from them. Changes are never easy to make, but they can be made with prayer and perseverance. We do not have to behave the same way our parents did. We have a choice.

Young marrieds do not have the long history that older families have. We middle agers should be able to glean interesting information by being with parents and siblings from both families.

If the parents are alive, take time to interact with them. Listen to and watch the parents of your financée. Talk to them about the son or daughter you are interested in marrying. They were there in the formative years. No one knows better the bents of that child, those attitudes and behaviors that make them who they are today in midlife.

Did You Marry a "Dead Family"?

What happens when you remarry a man or woman whose family of origin is dead? Answer: You are left with unanswered questions.

Couples marrying in midlife may or may not have the opportunity to meet and be with the parents prior to and during their marriage, depending on their age, health, or whether or not they are still alive.

When Bud and I married, my father had been dead fifteen years, and Bud's mother twenty-four. In the third year of our marriage, his father died. After his death I realized with a jolt that essentially I had married a "dead family." I would never hear from Bud's parents the joys and trials of raising him. I was not going to watch and listen to his parents communicate with one another and relate to one another, to see with my own eyes how living with those parents had contributed to the person Bud is today.

Neither would Bud see the kind of man my father was and learn what makes me tick where relationships with men are concerned. He could not have known that my father had a phlegmatic personality. He procrastinated and could not make decisions. His attitude was often, "I'll do it tomorrow—if I get around to it." Yet a main thrust to his life was peace. He did not enjoy strife. I have chosen men whose personalities are like his in many ways. Because I did not, however, like his "milquetoastishness" I have overcompensated in my own personality. I have strong opinions and make decisions quickly.

Except for my mother, our parents are gone. Because of being in our midlife Bud and I were unable to get acquainted with one another's parents. I often wonder how much like his mother he is. Without knowing his father for very long, I see how Bud is like him.

I had two brothers, and they are both dead, so my husband could not talk with a sibling to learn how I had grown up. Bud's sister, Diane, has shared lots of information with me about their growing-up years, and I am thankful for her insight and memories.

As I grow older I am amazed at the number of things that I do just as my mother did or does. When I was a teenager I swore (I took an oath) that I would never do and say the things she did. Today I find myself helplessly saying nearly the same words, posturing my body in the same way she did when she was my age, and probably even thinking similar thoughts. Others say they, too, hear themselves sounding just like one of their parents.

Is the person you are about to marry already looking and sounding like his father? Her mother? Look closely. Will you still love him when he has a paunch? Will you love her when she is wrinkled and has a double chin like her mother's? Will you love him when he's a "cantankerous old geezer"?

Other Secondary Relationships

Many other relationships populate the background of second marriages, making a human network to confront newly remarried people. When people divorce and remarry, or even when they are widowed and remarry, nobody really leaves the family system. You just add more people (See figure A).[3]

Your new spouse may have grown children and, if they are married, daughters- and sons-in-law. Grandchildren, and if you're old enough even great-grandchildren, may be part of a ready-made family. Add to that parents, siblings, aunts, uncles, cousins, brothers- and sisters-in-law, maybe even grandparents. Oh, and don't forget your and your previous spouse's families—those parents-in-law, sisters- and brothers-in-law, nieces and nephews who often play important roles in our lives, and we in theirs.

Beginning a marriage with this multitude of relationships already in place to figure out and keep in touch with can be a real burden for a newly married couple. Sometimes, frankly, it would be simpler not to try to build relationships. But Christians will do their best to get along with other people who come into their families. The Golden Rule is apropos here: "Do to others what you would have them do to you" (Matt. 7:12). No one likes to be ignored.

Let's face it, it will be important for everyone involved in a new stepfamily relationship to be on best behavior and

Figure A
Number of Interactions

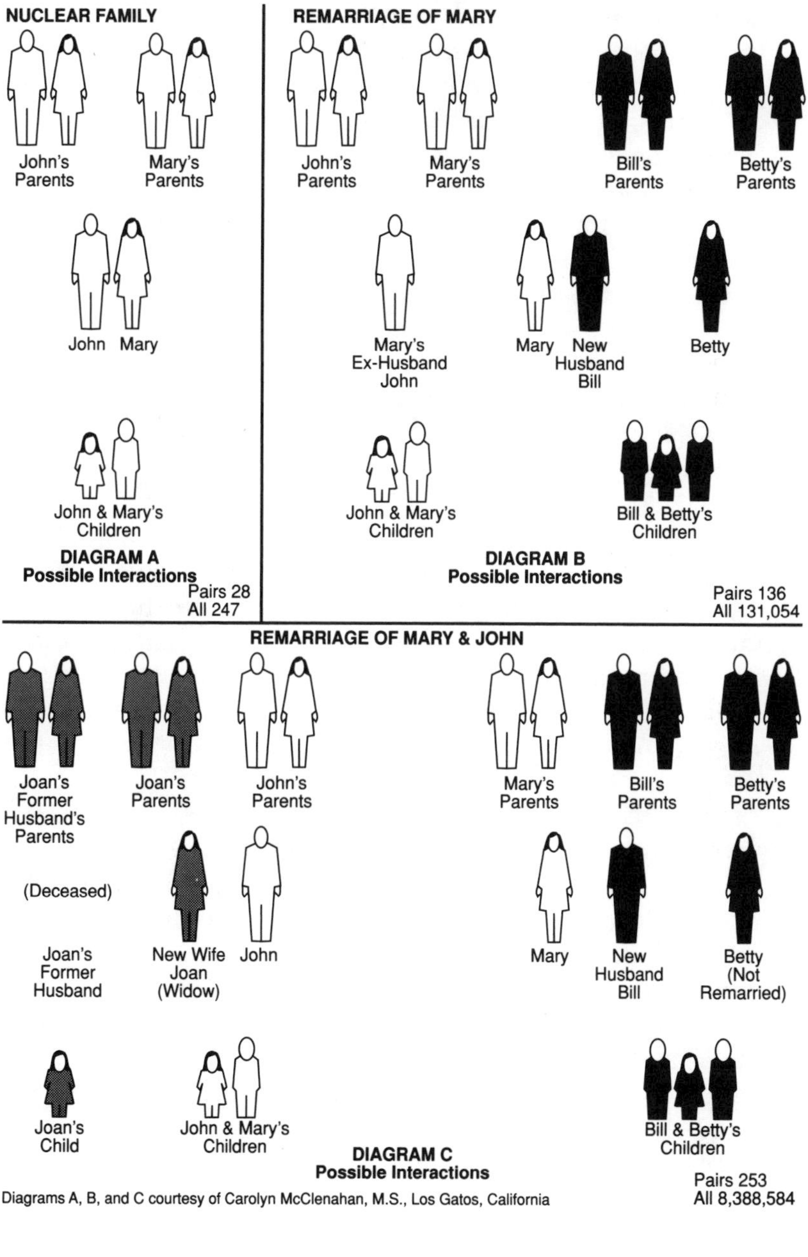

NUCLEAR FAMILY

John's Parents   Mary's Parents

John   Mary

John & Mary's Children

DIAGRAM A
Possible Interactions
Pairs 28
All 247

REMARRIAGE OF MARY

John's Parents   Mary's Parents   Bill's Parents   Betty's Parents

Mary's Ex-Husband John   Mary   New Husband Bill   Betty

John & Mary's Children   Bill & Betty's Children

DIAGRAM B
Possible Interactions
Pairs 136
All 131,054

REMARRIAGE OF MARY & JOHN

Joan's Former Husband's Parents   Joan's Parents   John's Parents   Mary's Parents   Bill's Parents   Betty's Parents

(Deceased)

Joan's Former Husband   New Wife Joan (Widow)   John   Mary   New Husband Bill   Betty (Not Remarried)

Joan's Child   John & Mary's Children   Bill & Betty's Children

DIAGRAM C
Possible Interactions
Pairs 253
All 8,388,584

Diagrams A, B, and C courtesy of Carolyn McClenahan, M.S., Los Gatos, California

make an effort to at least be polite and respectful to their new families.

In remarriage there is always the reverberation of "other people" who were, or are, part of a person's old life or former life. There are constant reminders from the past of others who came before you: photographs, monograms, laundry marks, furniture, tastes, and habits.

Sometimes I would like to throw away the clothing that was purchased by and given to my husband by his previous wife. Unfortunately, she had exquisite taste and bought only the very best quality. Some pieces, after more than twenty years, have only begun to wear out.

"His wife died," one woman said, "but the first six months of our marriage she was right there with us."

One man described how his ex-wife used to call and ask for a ride home from her late-evening job. "My wife often took the call and calmly told me that Millie needed a ride," he said. "I was astounded that she could be that caring, that she would encourage me to pick up my ex-wife and give her a ride. Finally we decided together that it wasn't the right thing to do. It just didn't look right to those who might see me driving her up the street. I encouraged her to find another ride."

In-law Relationships

Young couples usually have living mothers and fathers with whom they spend time during the early years of marriage and even when they have children. Many men and women develop wonderful relationships with their in-laws, loving them as much, sometimes more, than their birth parents.

I have such a relationship with my ex-mother-in-law. She is a good friend, and my husband enjoys her, too. We talk on the phone frequently, sharing prayers and concerns. She helps me clean my house twice a year and refuses to let me pay her. We laugh and cry together over funny and not-so-funny things. She has blessed my life with her love for God, her perseverance in times of darkness, and with her tremendous and zany sense of humor. I would have been the loser if I had not known her. Though my marriage to her son failed, my relationship with her has flourished for over thirty years.

What kind of in-law will you be? Are any of your children or stepchildren married? With two of Bud's children married, I am now twice a step-in-law. What are the criteria for that role? In-laws, particularly mothers-in-law, have gotten a bad rap over the years, much of it undeserving. Add *step* to that designation and you have a role to play in which the best possible solution is often silence, depending, of course, on the relationship between you and the stepchild. If that relationship is good, usually the stepchild's mate is accepting, too.

Acceptance is one thing everyone likes and usually expects from us. While this doesn't mean we must approve of all their particular behaviors, it comes under the heading of unconditional acceptance. All persons who come into our lives through remarriage have the right to be who God created them to be without someone trying to change them. Ruth Bell Graham said about her husband, "It's my job to love him. It's God's job to make him good." Love is our job in remarriages.

Often the emphasis is on younger persons treating parents-in-law with respect, which is good. But sometimes we older people think we have cornered the wisdom market; unless children and their spouses are willing to sit spellbound at our feet, we think they are hardheaded and ungrateful. Young people need to learn some of the same hard lessons that we did in our younger years. We have to be willing to step out of their way, giving them advice only when they ask for it.

In areas of disagreement, sometimes we are tempted to criticize different childrearing practices, lifestyles, or living arrangements. Remember that words left unsaid never have to be recalled. A quick read-through of James 3 on taming the tongue might give some nutritious food for

thought. Look for, no *search* for, the good in your in-laws
and step-in-laws and you will probably find it. When you
find it, magnify it.

Try not to let your concern for others be construed as
meddling. Concern is often best expressed directly to God
in prayer. "He who guards his mouth and his tongue keeps
himself from calamity" (Prov. 21:23). If you can put a muz-
zle on your mouth, you have a good chance to become a
beloved in-law rather than a dreaded out-law.

On the other hand, if your new mate's or intended's parents are still living, think how you will feel and respond if
they begin to give you advice.

One middle-aged man called his seventy-some-year-old
father to say he was planning to borrow money for some
home repairs, and wondered if his dad would like to have
the interest instead of the bank. "I had lived away from my
father for thirty-five years and had been quite successful,"
said Robert. "But instead of a yes or no, my dad only
wanted to give me advice." Borrowing money from family
members is sometimes fraught with danger. This grownups'
conversation ended with hard feelings, and the money was
not the issue.

As I put these suggestions into practice in my own
midlife remarriage, I hope that friendship and trust will be
the basis for my relationships with my stepchildren's mates
as well as with my own children's.

Grandparenting

There are many quotations from the pundits on grandparenting. "Grandchildren—all of the pleasures and none of
the problems." "God made it easy to love grandchildren.
They don't get you up at night." "If Mom says no and Dad
says no, ask Grandma." "Grandchildren are wonderful.
When you get tired of them you send them home." Most of
the quotations are fun. And grandchildren are fun, too.

"A child of your child is twice my child," is one of my
favorites. Ideally, grandchildren should be on the receiving

end of love from doting grandparents for the first years of their lives. Only when they are older does it become their responsibility to dote on their aging grandparents. How they do that and how much they do it will depend a great deal on grandparents' input into their lives in those early years.

Bud and I have two precious grandchildren as this book goes to press: little Megan, who is Bud's oldest son's child, and baby Jacob, who is my daughter's child.

We have had more chance to grandparent Jacob simply because he and his mommy are temporarily living with us, and because Megan lives a six-hour drive away. But we do not love one more or less than the other. In fact, we want our lives to be intertwined with our children's, and our grandchildren's.

We believe, however, that a necessary first adjustment must be made. We must give up parental authority and become our children's friends. A parent-friend relationship will help in the transformation to grandparent.

Our children need now to be considered as adults in their own right. As parents with young children we have more power because we need more power (along with wisdom). But in friendship with adult children there needs to be equality and mutuality. We need to assume that they can solve their own problems and if they can't, we probably can't do it for them.

So where does that leave grandparents? As lovers and encouragers, leaving a heritage that is much needed in our unstable world. Children need to know they are enjoyed, not just endured. Grandparents need to be caring, responsive, and emotionally available.

You may have been born and raised prior to the forties and fifties. You may remember simpler times and will undoubtedly have things you can share with your grandchildren that will carry on a heritage for them.

I can think of a number of games I played as a child that I am eager to teach Megan and Jacob someday—marbles and jacks and kick-the-can and hide-and-seek. And there will be walks in the timber discovering jack-in-the-pulpits and trilliums, "training" a special mushroom stick to hunt for the early spring morels that hide under the oak leaves, and walking in puddles after the rain.

When I think of the simplicity of my own school days and measure them against what is bombarding little ones' minds in today's public schools, from peers, and on TV, I realize the awesome responsibility I have to bring balance back into their lives.

Grandparents and grandchildren often live far away from one another. But the distance can still be bridged with frequent cards, letters, and talks by telephone or tape recorder Small gifts are fine, too, but children will remember the time you gave them more than the presents.

Even though Jacob is very small, Grandpa and I already love telling him stories. His eyes are expressive. He looks thrilled with our words. We think he understands. What matters is that we are communicating love.

The apostle Paul, in Titus 2, emphasizes the responsibility of older men and women to teach younger people. I consider that a blessed challenge—that as a grandparent, whether "real" or "step," I can share in the pleasure and training of the grandchildren. I am trusting that as I sow friendship and joy with them I will reap precious relationships.

And as with my children and my stepchildren, I have a responsibility as a Christian grandmother to lead the little ones or point them in the direction of Christ Jesus as Savior. The relationships that we build with our grandchildren here on earth are just the beginning of an eternal relationship.

That's the upside of grandparenting. There could be a downside. Not long ago I read a photo-story in our local newspaper about "recycled moms." The woman in the article was sixty years old and a full-time mother again. Because her daughter was unable to care for them, the woman was caring for two girls and two boys ages six to eleven, determined to keep them out of foster care.

How many other grandparents step in to raise their grandchildren? In Texas there is a statewide support group called Grandparents Raising Grandchildren. They estimate that nationwide about 3 percent of all children are being raised by grandparents.

One remarried grandparent couple in their eighties took the son of her daughter to raise when he was a hyperactive eleven-year-old after his mother died. People who knew his lifestyle before he went to live with Grandma say he is much better off. Now he gets regular meals, has consistent discipline, has been taken off of the drug Ritalin, and knows that he is loved and cared for. He is excelling in school and has learned to play a musical instrument for which he has pride, as do his grandparents.

Bud and I certainly did not talk about or plan to have a child and grandchild living with us, however temporarily. But there was a need, and we agreed to rise to it. If there was joy in our home before, it is bursting at the seams now. Jacob's life has made many changes in ours and in our relationships. We would never have guessed that God would use this unplanned baby in such major ways. We are thankful for his life.

Would you be prepared to do that in your remarriage, knowing that the child or children would not be blood relatives of one of you?

Custody of grandchildren outside of a court order creates other problems, such as health insurance or medical treatment without the signature or presence of a parent. How, in fact, do you get legal custody of a grandchild?

Some older men and women will not want to be involved with their grandchildren on a full-time basis. They enjoy the freedom to come and go on a moment's notice, especially if they are retired. Many midlifers are employed full time and simply are not available during the day to baby-sit.

"Marlin's daughter has the habit of calling him to say she will drop Billie off for the afternoon," said one frustrated instant stepgrandmother. "She never asks to speak to me. Then her dad goes off to his office, and I'm the one left to do the watching." This woman needs to communicate. For her to be still and allow this grownup child/woman to use her is incomprehensible. Nothing would be wrong with telephoning back and expressing herself: "Mary, your father has just told me you're planning to bring the baby for the afternoon. He's planning to be on the golf course this afternoon, and I already have plans, too. I'm sorry, it just won't work out for us to keep Billie today."

She might even suggest that Mary give them a little advance notice in the future to see if they are available. Too often men and women in stepfamily relationships are afraid that speaking the truth will damage an already tenuous relationship or will hurt the other person.

Open communication in all stepfamily relationships is a must. If each of you involved in remarriage or plans for a midlife remarriage will remember that one thing, at least you will know you have done your best to make the secondary relationships outside of your marriage work.

You cannot, however, assume that because you are a gifted communicator each of the stepchildren and other relatives will receive you warmly and with open arms, or that they will even consider your marriage to their divorced or widowed parent "real." If that is the case, wait on God and trust in him to work in your own life as well as in the lives of other family members.

6

Step Relationships:
Adult to Adult

Both Bud and I had waited ten and eleven years respectively after our divorces before remarriage. Still we wondered if we were ready for remarriage. We wonder if anyone ever is.

Did we know about the statistics? The dangers? We were not kids. We were already middle aged, or fast approaching it, depending on when you think people are middle aged.

Because three of our five children were out of high school and working or going to college, step relationships did not seem as critical to me as in remarriages with younger children. We had talked of waiting until our two daughters were out of high school before marrying, but friends had discouraged us from waiting.

"Foolish," one of them said. "It's your happiness. Why sacrifice your happiness for teenagers who will be wrapped up in their own lives and who will leave home soon anyway?"

It is true. When young people are ready to leave home,

they do not often look backward and say, "Poor old Mom. I can't go off to college. What would she do without me?"

So after a year of courtship we set the wedding date.

My husband is a pragmatist. He had reservations. I, on the other hand, believed that with God we could conquer anything. Most everyone liked me. And I had met no one who didn't think highly of Bud. Surely our kids would understand their parents' need of companions in their old age. I guess I used my persuasive abilities on Bud.

What is it, do you suppose, that happens to men and women in love? We seem willing, yes, even eager, to avoid facts and statistics and leap into the fray. I admit it; I was blinded by midlife love, liberally laced with unrealistic idealism.

People asked me if my husband's children accepted me.

"They will," I chirped. "I'll love them and everything will work out. Besides," I blathered on in blissful happiness, "they're older. They'll all be away from home soon." And I believed my kids would accept Bud, too. What could possibly be a problem?

Somewhere in my fantasy I believed that older children would not pose any problems for our remarriage. Having their own careers and relationships, they would have their own stresses to deal with.

Little Children, Little Problems; Big Children, Big Problems

Many people find this aphorism all too true. Remarriage, even after awareness of the pitfalls and careful planning to avoid them, is still a challenge. Psychologist Margaret Doren says,

> The interpersonal problems in a remarriage are even greater than if it were just two kids getting married for the first time. Establishing a marriage relationship *and* a parent relationship at the same time is extremely difficult because you are adjusting to a whole family relationship, perhaps five,

six or seven new and different people. The problems are squared, not just multiplied.[1]

If you think there won't be problems, your thinking is erroneous. So will be your expectations. You can almost count on fireworks when families with adult children merge. The stepparent has not been involved in the childhood training. The stepparent has often come into the other parent's life after the children have had years of quality "alone" time with their parent.

Grown children and grown parents are both capable of bad behavior in a remarriage-stepfamily relationship. One never-married woman who married a divorced man with children made it very clear before their marriage that she wanted nothing to do with her husband's children, no matter what! She has remained true to her vow. And it has surely caused problems in their marriage. We hope vows of that nature are a minority.

Another stepmother happily accepts, even expects, her husband's kindnesses to *her* college-age children from a previous marriage. But when *his* children come, she goes to her room, shutting herself away from them.

Stepfamilies: A Fact of Life

Current estimates are that more than a third of all children born in the 1980s will experience a parental divorce before age eighteen.[2] With some divorce statistics indicating a 50 percent failure rate for marriages, it is no wonder that stepfamilies are more and more in the news.

By 1995 it is predicted that stepfamilies will outnumber traditional families. More spouses will be part of a remarriage than a first marriage, and one of every five children may be living with a stepparent.

Census Bureau predictions make it seem inevitable: of every 100 children born in 1983, 12 were born out of wedlock; 40 will live in a family where there is at least one divorce; 5 will experience a prolonged parental separation;

and 2 will experience the death of a parent. Only 41 of the 100 will be reared in a traditional setting with a mother and father. This means that 59 of every 100 children will likely live in a stepfamily before age 18.

Studies recently done on children of divorce have yielded information that surprises some people. Judith Wallerstein, a secular psychologist, studied for more than a decade 60 divorced families which included 131 children. She has now written the book *Second Chances*, which describes the adult hope for a better marriage the second time around.

But the children's perspective is compelling. One controversial conclusion in her book is that "almost half of the children entered adulthood as worried, underachieving, self-deprecating and sometimes angry young men and women."[3]

Wallerstein calls divorce a "man-woman crisis," which they resolve when one marital chapter is closed and they go on to the next one. But the children don't operate in chapters. The children are looking to man-woman relationships for guidance in who they will be in adulthood.

Perhaps that explains, from a worldly perspective, why people from broken homes and marriages have problems in their own marriages and relationships. Perhaps that expresses some of the ambivalence that stepchildren, no matter what their age, have for their new stepmothers or stepfathers.

These people will always be stepchildren and their birth parent's mate will always be a stepparent. No amount of tinkering will change them into biological kids.

I used to feel anger at the authorities who used neat words such as *blended* to describe families created by a marriage that combines two sets of children into one household. It gave a "pink-cloud," optimistic expectation of perfect happiness and cohesiveness.

Blended conjured in my mind a picture of ingredients in the mixing bowl that, being stirred together, made something tasteful and wonderful. According to *Webster's New World Dictionary,* Third College Edition, *blend* means "to mix and mingle; to mix thoroughly; to merge; to harmonize; a mixture of varieties."[4]

The last, "a mixture of varieties," best described our "blended" family in its early years. But it didn't blend. Ours was like oil and water. The two don't mix.

Call stepfamilies whatever you will, they are definitely structurally different from biological families. They have been called other names such as *reorganized, combined, melded, reconstituted,* and *synergistic.* Some have called them all mixed up. Doris Jacobson, a researcher from UCLA, has coined the term *linked family system* to describe two families who "share" a child.

Just the number of labels gives some idea of the confusion in defining the group. While stepfamilies do not work like The Brady Bunch, neither are they made up of the myths embodied in *Cinderella* and *Snow White.*

Whatever they are, they are unique and must not be considered to be like or expected to act like the traditional family. The mature man or woman who goes into a remarriage that includes children, no matter how old they are, and thinks they will have an immediate close relationship is having a pipe dream.

"One woman felt her stepchildren resented her because she took better care of them than their own mother did," writes Leslie Westoff, author of *Second Time Around,* "but surely she would have been resented just as much if she neglected them."[5]

Stepfamily Myths

"Three popular myths about stepfamilies interfere with realistic expectations," says Mary Lou Fuller, associate professor at the University of North Carolina.[6]

"Myth 1: Stepfamily members' roles are identical to roles in traditional families."[7]

This myth does not change with the age of the child nor with the length of time a stepfamily sticks together.

However, I can truthfully say that it does get better with time and effort.

With the struggles to get acquainted and like one another that Bud and I had with each other's children and they with us, both of us are pleased with the growth to date. Having only two of our children married has kept the number of relationships fairly static. Our daughter-in-law and son-in-law are special people to have as part of the family. Our grandchildren are like icing on the cake. We see how little people can have a positive effect on families.

Recently when I opened the mail I found a Mother's Day greeting and a gift from Megan to Nana. Another card addressed to "Helen" and signed "Love Kevin and Suzanne" won the "Blessing of the Day" prize. It was a day to rejoice in God's abundant goodness. But first I had to cry a bit.

"Myth 2: Instant Love."[8]

Mothers expect to love their newborn babies instantly. Some do not, however, and express the fear and ambivalence they feel about the tiny person who is totally dependent on them.

Then comes a remarriage, and somehow we think we are to instantly love someone else's child with that same kind of love. It's a setup! Planted in the same hill with the expectations are bound to grow disappointment, guilt, and resentment.

"In sheer self-defense," said one woman, "my attitude had to be 'You're not my kids. You have a mother and a father.' I hoped that one day they would have respect and maybe even affection for me."

When we consider the time involved in learning to love and accept one another in a midlife remarriage, it is not reasonable to assume that all of the adult children, their mates, and their children will experience instant love for the stepparent.

It takes time—a lot of time—for feelings of love to develop. Prayer will help. Sometimes it is difficult to like a new stepparent or a grown stepchild—especially when one can be obstreperous. But respect rubs off.

Ask God to love through you. Some days you will say, "I simply can't do it." God specializes in the impossible. He has you where he wants you. He loves to work through your weaknesses.

"Myth 3: Stepfamilies function just like traditional families."[9]

Traditional families are tied together by blood lines. They are family in the purest sense of the word—a mother, a father, and children born from the union and love of those two.

With the advent of the hippie movement in the 1960s people began to think of a family as any persons who lived together, whether married or not. In fact, *Webster's New World Dictionary,* Third College Edition identifies a family as a "household establishment; all the people living in the same house" in its first definition.[10]

Stepfamilies, while not family in the purest sense, are the combination of the husband and wife and *their* families, bringing into the circle people from various backgrounds and blood lines. Because of this, they function differently. Friendships and relationships are often harder to build.

What Is a Christian Stepparent's Responsibility?

An old Chinese proverb says, "Govern your family as you would cook a small fish—very gently."

This proverb certainly expresses the care needed when building relationships in a remarriage that includes adult children.

I found that I had to work my way through the maze of hurts before I could begin to discover what God's plan was for me in the role of a stepparent.

Does Scripture offer a guideline in these circumstances? While it is not specific, look at Joseph and his brothers. They were all fathered by the same man, but birthed by several different mothers. Even with a common father, these children had trouble getting along. Why would we think it would be easy for children from different fathers *and* mothers to get along?

After a year or two I found and attended several support group sessions with a licensed stepfamily counselor who periodically held workshops for stepparents and stepchildren. The group at least gave me the security that I was not the only person struggling with stepparenting relationships. The vast majority of the couples however, had small children of preschool and grade school age from one or both of their marriages, whom they were trying to meld into family units—not adult children with careers and families of their own.

Our five children by this time ranged in age from sixteen to twenty-three. Their personalities were intact with all the strengths and weaknesses that every adult possesses—needs, habits, problems. We did believe, however, that we could still have a positive influence on them.

Dos and Don'ts for Stepparents

After ten years, I have come up with several things that a stepparent with adult stepchildren should and should not do.

The first on the list bears consideration before a remarriage.

1. *Do not* try to make your children love your intended mate as much as you do, either before you marry or after. To you he may be a super hero or she may be Super Woman. You can be sure he will not be to your children. If you exaggerate your prospective mate's attributes, you set him or her up for failure in the eyes of your children.

They probably already have unrealistic expectations, and you unknowingly may be forcing your intended into a role that will be impossible to fulfill.

You will probably not be "one big happy family." Each person must figure out what his or her role is—often a long, complicated, and painful process akin to organ transplant. The host family may reject the newcomer as alien tissue.

2. *Do* accept whatever level of closeness your grown family and your new mate are willing to give one another. Remember the instant love myth? Giving and receiving "perfect" love is difficult, if not impossible, for even the most godly person. In a new integrated family it is unrealistic.

3. *Do not* blame the children for things that go wrong in your marriage. Your marriage is your marriage. You and your mate may make the choice to be in control of your own relationship. When problems arise, you may feel a tendency to put blame on someone outside of your marriage (your wife seems to be airing the family's problems with her son on the phone, or your husband says having your daughter around all the time is causing the problems in your marriage) but don't do it! Somewhere the channels of communication have broken down. Perhaps someone other than your mate has taken that number-one place in your life.

4. *Do* seek wisdom from God in those instances where you are tempted to take sides with a child, or to feel sorry for a grownup who feels slighted by your new mate. Spend time in prayer and in God's Word seeking help in every situation. You do *not* want to get in the middle. Let each person in your new family be responsible for his or her own feelings and communication. Provide support to both mate and child.

5. *Do not* hold back anger at a stepchild if there is a reason to express anger. But remember that anger often comes from a judgmental spirit and is often used to control others. Be reasonable while you are expressing anger. Yelling is not okay. As in any family situation, accusing tears people down and tends to break down communication rather than improve it. The apostle Paul says it better than I can say it: "Therefore each of you must put off falsehood and speak truthfully to his neighbor, for we are all members of one body. In your anger do not sin. Do not let the sun go down while you are still angry, and do not give the devil a foothold" (Eph. 4:25–27).

Unexpressed anger almost always comes out sideways and gets on innocent people. In addition, enough studies conclude that anger not dealt with in healthy ways ends up harming the angry one, creating stress and ulcers, not to mention the loss of joy in Jesus Christ.

6. *Do* involve each person in your stepfamily in some way. Teach a skill, spend time shopping, share a good book, and give compliments and encouragement—lots of it. "Our words should be like little silver boxes with a bow on top," says Florence Littauer in her book *Silver Boxes*.[11]

It has been fun to discover favorites that my new family members have and prepare special foods for them. One Christmas season I ran into a good buy on small red buckets with lids. The nifty bonus was that a talented painter was on duty who monogrammed each bucket with a kid's name. I then filled the buckets with favorite cookies or candies.

Most of all, listen. Learn when and how to communicate with these new people in your life. A wise person once noted that it was no accident that God created us with one mouth and two ears.

7. *Do not* overdo. It is tempting to try too hard to please. Give these grownups space. Dissatisfaction accumulates like dust. Sometimes we are tempted to sweep it under the rug. But eventually the pile gets so big that it's noticeable and must be cleaned out. Holding on to small items of discontent can lead to large caches of anger. How much better to handle them as they come.

8. *Do* express your values and ideas, but be sensitive; not everyone will see things as you do. Build a godly home. "As for me and my household, we will serve the LORD" (Josh. 24:15). Show your families a relaxed good time when they are in your home. Give family members supplements of warmth, knowledge, friendship, and faith. And always support your mate wholeheartedly as master or mistress of your home.

9. *Do not* let yourself be lured by baits such as "you this" and "my dad that." It is perfectly okay while you are getting acquainted with your new family to keep responses indefinite while at the same time not taking the bait.

One man told of a grown stepchild who enjoyed baiting

him about his faith in God. Comments such as, "Is that how a Christian behaves?" or "That sure isn't Christian" were commonplace. He kept his tongue, showing peace rather than taking the bait and responding with words that would only confirm the accusations.

10. *Do* be yourself. You are not their mother or father. You never will be. But one day you may be their friend. How much better to be who you really are than to begin a game of pretend.

11. *Never* criticize the other parent. Not only is it not godly, but it will drive a wedge. Even when the stepchildren complain or speak negatively about their own parents, never get involved. Only uplift and uphold them with compliments and encouragement.

Multiple Families, Multiple Homes

Couples who marry in midlife often have family members living under several different roofs. In our case, at the time of our marriage we had one of his and one of mine living with us, one living with her mother, one in his own apartment in town, and one living in Minnesota. Now, ten years later, our house is usually empty of children; at different times three of the singles have come home to roost for a few months. Right now they are living in four different states.

Adult siblings have trouble getting acquainted with the children of their parents' mates. Sometimes there is no opportunity to get acquainted. Other times there simply is no inclination.

When my own mother remarried, I was twenty-six years old and had a family of my own. Her husband's children were also grown and had families. My mother did not try to get us together and combine us as a family, although I'm sure it would have been okay.

After my mother and stepfather were married for over twenty years, my stepfather's daughter and I began a relationship. During one of her hospital stays I had given her a book of Christian fiction that made a dramatic change in her life. We had two years of friendship with one another before her early death. I am thankful that I was able to share my Lord with her. I am sure she is in heaven with him now.

With our grown children I have made an effort to combine the two families at Thanksgiving, Easter, and Christmas when they are apt to be back in town for vacations or visits. Plans must be flexible. Sometimes it works. Other times it doesn't.

Multiple Agendas

All the people involved in a stepfamily come with their own agendas. Some drag the heavy baggage we mentioned earlier—the hurts and memories of the past. Their undying wish is that their "real" mother and daddy could have made it work.

One woman expressed her initial hurt when she visited her stepdaughter's home and found numerous photos of her mother and father together. Her hurt turned to sorrow for the young woman though, when she realized that even as an adult she had not let go of the hope that her father and mother may still get together.

Feelings are always an issue in adult stepfamilies. Even in families where several members of the new stepfamily system are Christians, feelings of anger, resentment, jealousy, and downright hostility are apt to be factors—no matter how we try to conceal it, no matter how godly we are.

I considered it my responsibility as a Christian to show God's love to my stepchildren. As time went by, God gave me feelings of real love for each one of them.

Setting a tone of peace and an atmosphere of love in our home was important to me. Allowing all of our children to see a positive relationship between my husband and me was highest on the list. Even after previous marriage failures, we believed it was not too late to let our marriage relationship speak for itself to our kids. Our unspoken goal was that they should see us happy together.

Often the worst effects of parents' divorce, no matter how long ago it was, can be muted by their willingness to include grown stepchildren into their new families. Remember, it may have been years since children of divorced parents came together as a family for a special celebration of a birthday or another holiday.

My children and I were big on celebrations. It didn't take much for us to plan a party, bake a cake, have friends in. But Bud, during the time he lived alone, seldom went to the trouble to put up a Christmas tree or to plan holidays with his children. Perhaps that's a womanly kind of thing. At any rate, I believe his children were glad to have holiday celebrations again, even if there was an "outsider" involved.

One thing is certain: It is never right to pretend feelings that aren't there. Everyone sees through it. There were times in our first years of marriage that I had to leave the room because I could not participate in the conversation. I could not pretend that I agreed. I also learned that I did not always have to be right.

Respect for each child's individuality and private life is a must. Parents know there are times we disagree with what our children do. But we don't stop loving them. It is no different with stepchildren. And the same treatment applies: Love the person, hate the behavior.

Stepparents make mistakes the same as stepchildren. I'm an inveterate letter writer. I have, for many years, written a Christmas newsletter that is mailed to our friends all over the country. It has been a real challenge to make the letter a combined letter that tells my friends about my children and Bud's old friends about his children.

One year I innocently wrote something about one of Bud's children I assumed was common knowledge; but it wasn't. Oh, how I wish I hadn't! And the anger directed at me was justified. I was wrong and admitted it. I was humbled and asked forgiveness. I was forgiven and the episode,

I believe, opened the door to better understanding. Even painful mistakes can lead to more meaningful relationships.

One of the most important responsibilities for a Christian stepparent is prayer. Whether or not stepchildren or step-siblings are Christians, there is nothing more personal and loving that one can do than to pray for them.

Christmas of 1987 was one of the most frustrating and yet interesting of my life. A crisis in the lives of a couple of our young adult children had precipitated hope for some needed changes. Because my husband dislikes conflict and goes out of the way to avoid it, he went to our cottage for a few days by himself to sort out his thoughts and feelings. So Bud was not going to be home on Christmas Eve or Christmas Day.

Once I might have been devastated enough to cancel Christmas. Instead, because I was secure in the grace of God and knew my husband's need for a time alone, I forged ahead to have as interesting and enjoyable, if unusual Christmas.

I called my husband's children and told them their father had decided he needed some time by himself, that he was heading for Lake O'Dessa.

"You are more than welcome to come for Christmas Eve dinner as planned," I said. "But if you decide not to because your dad isn't here, I will understand."

They all came. I assured them that it wasn't about any-thing they had said or done, and showed by my own accep-tance of the situation that everything was okay. We all had a delightful time.

Stepchildren's Responsibilities

"I wouldn't have chosen him or her, but . . . ." That state-ment is made numerous times by men and women whose parent married when they were older, making them adult stepchildren.

I was pleased when my own mother remarried. It was a relief to know that she had someone she cared for and who cared for her, someone with whom to spend time and go places. While I knew her husband would never replace my father, still I cared for him.

Other grown children feel differently. Some of them sit in judgment of their parent's choice of a mate. As we will show in the next chapter, "Expecting Problems," that judgment can be made very clear in hurtful ways.

My daughter was ambivalent about my remarriage. She would have preferred that I remain single. Her attitude was, We don't need a man; things are fine the way they are.

Of all the members of both of our families, she was the one who made the most changes—new school, different community, different room, new friends, new church, and leaving her brother and all of her friends behind. None of the other children left their familiar surroundings.

In the eighth year of our marriage she began a relationship with my husband. It took some honesty on my part to open the window of possibility. Sara had invited me to one of her counseling sessions, where I revealed the hurt I felt when she came home and did not include Bud in the conversations.

Her counselor was able to say to Sara, "Would that be too hard for you? Couldn't *you* make the effort to reach out to Bud and greet him when you go home?"

Bless her heart. She made the choice to be pleasant and respectful. The doors opened. The light came in. It only took one person to decide. There had been an eight-year stalemate. Now it was broken, and a relationship ensued. Both Bud and Sara discovered there could be stimulating conversations, that each of them had good sense and something to offer the other.

Now, a couple of years later, Sara is home with us with her son, Jacob. And now the little one opens the doors to all kinds of wonderful communication.

"There are countless other examples of decisions which all of us face at one time or another," said Elizabeth Skoglund in her book *Growing Through Rejection.* "To put it

in the colloquial: 'We can't win.' Rejection and misunderstanding are inevitable. The only answer is to commit one-
self to the course which seems right and to rest in one's
rightness with God rather than feel defeated by any rejection which may come from man."[12]

January 4, 1988

The New Year! The glitter and trim of Christmas had
been put away. Everyone had gone home. The reality of a
still-fragmented family was plain.

As I sat in my studio that morning I cried out to the Lord,
"O God, do you not hear me? I have begged you on behalf
of our children and this family for eight years. I have
pleaded with you to bring these young people to you. Lord,
when will you hear my prayer?"

In the quiet, I heard the words of a song (my radio was
playing softly in the background): "Don't give up on the
brink of a miracle. Don't give up, God is still on the
throne."

That afternoon, God worked a miracle. Bud's daughter,
Jennifer, came to our home, and I led her in prayer to
receive Christ as her personal Savior.

I share this story to give the reader hope. God *is* still on
his throne and he *is* in control of every situation in your
family and mine. If we as Christian stepparents and
stepchildren will yield to him, if we will pray and trust the
Lord, we will see harvests of righteousness.

Don't stop praying for your family to be used for God's
glory.

7

Expect Problems

Everything was not hunky-dory and it was clear almost immediately in our marriage. The gray cloud of previous failures hung just within my eyesight causing me to question my capabilities as a wife and mother.

I had believed that being a Christian, trusting God and his Word, loving my new husband with all my heart, plus the love and understanding of other believers would see me through the adjustment time in this remarriage.

One woman whom I met at a Christian conference just "happened" to reveal in conversation that she was experiencing rejection from her husband's grown children. Besides that, her husband was intolerant and unloving toward her grown children from her previous marriage.

This kind of rejection and hurt certainly is not unique. Nor is it isolated. There are undoubtedly many other Christian (and certainly non-Christian) adult stepfamilies who are going through similar problems—maybe stuck in them.

"All families experience stressful times. Children tend to show little day-to-day appreciation for their parents, and at times they get angry and reject their natural parents," writes E. B. Visher. "But the mixture of feelings can be even more intense in stepfamilies than in intact families."[1]

Statistics show that young stepmothers with stepchildren under ten years of age tend to develop close relationships, though each family situation is unique.

"On the other hand," writes Bobbie Reed, author of *Stepfamilies Living in Christian Harmony,* "blended families where both mates have adolescents are the least successful for the obvious reasons. The greatest period of stress for a biological family is the children's adolescence. Combining two adults and one or more adolescents from two different families to form a new family is to attempt stepkinship under the most adverse conditions possible."[2]

While I might have wished for Reed's book before marriage, the problem she described with adolescents was not new information. I expected normal challenges and problems from both of our girls; they were classic adolescents when we married. We were not disappointed!

But the boys did not fit any textbook description. They were older. There seemed to be no helpful book about the relationships between stepparents and grown children in their early to late twenties, or even really grown children in their thirties and forties.

The person who said, "If the future is so rosy, why am I feeling so blue?" expressed how the remarried person feels when the problems and challenges with the new stepfamily begin.

"Stepparents are, in a fundamental sense, unwanted parents," said Brenda Maddox, author of *The Half-Parent.* "Research shows that children do not easily accept substitute parents and that there is more discord and tension in stepfamilies than in ordinary families."[3]

Maddox was referring more to young children in stepfamilies than to those who are older teens or even selfsupporting young adults who are away from home. "As a stepfamily settles in, tests run the gamut from defiance . . . to manipulation, to outright rejection," says Elizabeth Einstein.[4]

"Nothing is more destructive to a person than repeated rejection," says Gerald L. Dahl. "Eventually that person finds it nearly impossible to trust *anyone*, even though the desire and basis for trust may be there."[5]

No one has ever suffered more rejection and emotional insult than Jesus. He was rejected, lied against, and people he counted on turned away from him. He was betrayed by close friends. Even his mother did not understand him. He was abused physically and, even more, emotionally. And it was all undeserved.

Often the rejection in stepfamilies is not deserved, either. Nevertheless, we can count on it. And it hurts. Much of the rejection comes for reasons that have nothing to do with the person being rejected. It usually comes from the frustrations and fears of the person who is striking out—fear of the unknown, fear of change, fear of being unloved.

On the other hand, stepparents or stepchildren who have unrealistic expectations of the new family member will feel rejection when things do not go the way they had planned or expected. While perhaps rejection in these instances is not deserved, realizing what set us up to be rejected and changing *our* behavior can help some to alleviate the hurt.

Two Varieties of Rejection

Under the heading of undeserved rejection I have arrived at two varieties: overt rejection, which comes out in open hostility, and covert rejection, the hidden or disguised kind of rejection that often seems more hurtful.

Overt Rejection

When children are small and unafraid of saying what they think, they might kick the new stepparent in the shins and say, "I don't like you. I don't want you to be my mommy (or daddy)." They might even be more forceful and honest and say, "I hate you! I don't want you to come live with us."

Most adults can deal with that kind of openness and honesty. After you get over the initial shock of being told to "take a hike," at least you know where you stand and that you have a place to begin a relationship. At the bottom.

Everyone knows the Bible story of Joseph. He is remembered as a blameless man who was "done dirty" by his half-brothers and who many years later reminded them, "You intended to harm me, but God intended it for good" (Gen. 50:20).

One rereading of Genesis 37 will give you a picture of a teenager who is bringing tattle-tale information to his father about his half-brothers. "Joseph, a young man of seventeen, was tending the flocks with his brothers . . . and he brought their father a bad report about them" (Gen. 37:2). These accounts were not designed to bring harmony in the Jacob family.

Children and parents both know that when they bring "bad reports" about their stepsiblings or about the stepparent, there are bound to be repercussions.

The other problem we see is that Joseph's father showed favoritism to him overtly by making him "a richly ornamented robe."

What happened is predictable. "When his brothers saw that their father loved him more than any of them, they hated him and could not speak a kind word to him" (Gen. 37:4). We can assume one of two things: Either they ignored him and said nothing to him, which would be covert rejection, or more probably, they told him regularly how much they hated him. Overt rejection.

Was it Joseph's fault they hated him because of the robe his father made for him? No, their anger was misplaced and undeservingly given to Joseph. In fairness and honesty Israel's sons should have approached their father and told him how they felt at seeing his favoritism of Joseph.

But in Genesis 37:5 we begin to see how Joseph created problems for himself because of his superior attitude. After hearing his dream, "his brothers said to him, 'Do you intend to reign over us? Will you actually rule us?' And they hated him all the more because of his dream and what he had said." When Joseph had his next dream, where the sun, the moon, and the stars bowed down to him, his brothers were jealous of him.

Joseph's subsequent sale to the Midianite merchants by his brothers may be the private desire of many stepsiblings or stepparents, but hopefully we can discover better solutions to the jealousy and hatred that children and parents alike feel toward their new family members.

His overt rejection by them was undeserved, no matter how jealous and angry Joseph's stepbrothers were.

Covert Rejection

Unfortunately many adults, both stepparents and stepchildren, do not play as straight as Israel's unfavored sons. They hide their feelings of anger and resentment inside. They ignore. They spurn any overtures of friendship or warmth. And all of this can be done without words. They have subtle yet painful ways of getting their point across.

Covert rejection is perhaps the most familiar to adolescents, older children, and adults. It is the underhanded, insidious kind of rejection where one is hurt without words or overt action. It is hard to pin down, the kind that you cannot confront without seeming to be paranoid.

Sometimes the rejector has no conscious awareness of what he is doing to reject. Other times he does know. It is secret service, undercover meanness, that is a carefully calculated and deadly serious game designed to hurt and maim, perhaps kill. Most certainly its purpose is to sabotage the remarriage.

This is the kind of rejection that is tearing stepfamilies apart, because it is so hard to confront. It takes honesty and a willingness to make changes to stop it.

Rejection Games

Every person, parents and children alike, involved in a stepfamily relationship probably plays some kind of rejec-

tion game. Here are a few that members of stepfamilies
have become adept at recognizing. (Because there is a positive and beautiful side to stepfamilies, in the next chapter
we shall cover "How to Handle Problems and Survive.")

1. *Divide and conquer.* In this game the child (whether
young or old) works to alienate his or her biological parent
from the new spouse. It can work from both sides of the
relationship. The child determines to approach each adult
separately, or the child makes derogatory remarks about the
stepparent to the biological parent.

John realized that when his daughter came to the house
to visit she would get him or his wife alone to talk. But
when the other person came into the room, she would stop
talking. His daughter was willing to go places with John *or*
with his wife, but she declined any invitation to go with
them as a couple. She did not want to—or she was not
ready to—be part of a three-person family relationship.

This method of rejection can usually be overcome with
time. As adult stepchildren see their parent and the new
mate relating in love to one another, they will come to
acceptance and will begin to feel more comfortable including the new husband or wife in their conversations.

Interestingly, in a traditional family roles are assigned or
ascribed. Mom is a mom because she bore the child. In
stepfamilies roles are achieved. They are earned through
individual effort.

From another angle, Denise reported that her mother
had been married to her stepfather for over twenty-five
years. "Each year our relationship gets more difficult," says
Denise. "As he has aged, he has become more disagreeable.
If Mother calls when he is in the house, sometimes I can
hear him yell in the background, 'Why are you calling her?
She doesn't need to know where we're going.'" Even adults
work at dividing and conquering.

Denise expressed the hurt and rejection she feels. Her
stepfather's children have paid very little attention to his
and her mother's needs. She has been the one who assists
whenever anything is needed. While she does it without

expecting anything in return, she finds it painful to receive the rejection.

2. *If I ignore him maybe he'll go away.* This is a familiar rejection to most people in step relationships. It is hard for any parents to believe that their grown children, who have been trained to be polite and considerate of others, could be so skilled at treating others as though they did not exist.

One woman said that before her remarriage she and her children spent time at the dinner table each evening sharing happenings of their day at work and school. "So when Bill and I married, my daughter continued to talk about her day," she said. "The only problem was that she left Bill out of the conversation. She talked to me. She looked at me."

Treating persons as though they don't exist is an insidious and painful form of rejection. It hurts so badly it is as damaging as physical abuse.

One woman married a widower and began raising his four-year-old daughter as her own child, loving and training her through the formative years, only to have the child begin doubting her mother love in her adolescent years.

When the daughter left home she rejected this woman she had known as mother since her toddler years. Pictures of her long-dead mother were displayed all over her house. There was certainly nothing wrong with having pictures of her birth mother, but pictures of the only mother she had ever known were nowhere to be seen.

The mother described the torment of supposing she should have been big enough to display the child's biological mother's picture in their home when she and her husband were newly married. At the time, however, she believed it was best for her marriage and for her new relationship with the four-year-old not to.

3. *Eye for an eye, tooth for a tooth.* This kind of rejection is often the defense mechanism to if-I-ignore-him-maybe-he'll-go-away rejection. It says without words, "I'll give you back a dose of your own medicine." And no one wins.

The woman whose daughter ignored her stepfather was caught between these two rejection varieties when her husband was hurt by her daughter's chatter at the dinner table. Instead of confronting her with his hurt, he responded with an ill-natured sulk.

"In the early days of our marriage I was a full-blown fixer," she said, "and felt totally responsible for his discomfort as well as my daughter's."

She relates that dinner hours are much more pleasant now that they have all learned to honestly express their feelings.

4. Roller coaster. Shirley described how her relationship with a stepson in his midtwenties changed directions as quickly as a Yo-Yo. She felt cared for and a necessary part of the family one day. Another day, often the very next, she was ignored and disliked.

"My emotions were on a roller coaster," she said. "I tried to figure out his system. Was it odd days or even days when he liked me? Maybe it was warm days. Cold days?" She laughed, then added, "Finally I began to realize the principles I had learned in the Alanon fellowship years earlier could also apply to this no-win relationship. Unfortunately it took me years of anguish to remember what I knew about detaching from the problem, not the person."

5. Killing them softly with silence. This form of rejection is closely akin to "If I ignore him . . . " except it is more overt.

Several men and women told stories about times when their stepchildren had left them in a deafening silence, the kind that says, "You are a nonperson."

"It might seem like simple inconsideration to the casual onlooker," said Julie, "but this kind of treatment was commonplace when my stepdaughter was around."

One woman described a stepchild's long distance telephone etiquette. If she answered the phone, she heard, "Is Mr. Brown there?" Not: "Is my father there?" which is a mean enough rebuff. She would reply, "Hi, Cindy, yes, I'll get your father for you." It became a sick game they played.

Another man said he felt unspoken anger from an adult stepchild because he had "taken her mother away from her." "But there was *never* a conversation when direct disappointment or anger could be dealt with," he said. "Instead, I always felt as though I had been slapped in the face for some unknown reason."

"It came to a head one day," he continued, "and both of us got our messages across." It was true the grown daughter had felt as though this man had stolen her mother away from her.

He pointed out that her mother and he had chosen each other. "If your attitude is hurting me, it is fair to assume that it is also very painful to your mother," he said. Her attitude began to change.

Even older children can feel they have lost a parent to a remarriage. Often addressing the situation up front can open the doors to improved communication in the future.

6. *Disappearing act or cyclical rejection.* Some families see their children (both real and step) on a regular basis, whether it is daily, weekly, or regularly on holidays.

One couple described how they had a child living in the same city who would drop in and eat a meal, who would occasionally come for weeks or months on a daily or several-times-a-week basis, seemingly working at relating to both his father and his father's wife. Then for no apparent reason the young man would disappear for three, six, or twelve months. During that time there might not be even a telephone call. Then one day, like a recurring event, he would appear again.

7. *I don't want your help.* Kindnesses as small as the offer of a cup of coffee or a glass of water receive a cold refusal from this person. Within five minutes, however, the person will get the cup of coffee or the glass of water for himself or herself. This rejection of kindness or service seems to say, "I refuse to be thankful for anything you give me or do for me."

Invitations of any kind are spurned or if they are accepted are often not kept.

"There were any number of times," said Debbie, "when my stepson came by after work to talk to his dad for a minute, and I would suggest setting another place at the table.

"'No thanks, I have to get going,' he would answer. Only he would linger and linger, until finally we would go ahead and sit down to eat. When we were nearly through, he would get out a plate and eat standing up."

8. Sibling interference. When there is more than one child in a family, often one of them will begin to relate to a stepparent before the others do. This occasionally prompts a reverse kind of jealousy in other siblings.

"When I began to draw close to my new stepmother," said Brenda, "one of my brothers warned me that I'd better not do that because I would hurt my mom."

Loyalty issues and the laying of guilt trips indicate a lack of security with the biological parent. If the daughter (or son) who is becoming comfortable with her new relationship succumbs to the sibling's pressure tactics and backs off from the new relationship, she will suffer from double guilt.

9. Previous spouse rejection. On the other hand, there are biological parents who are insecure and have a terrifying fear that their child, no matter what the age, will love a stepparent more than themselves.

Many people described the trouble that can be brought to bear by their previous mates, particularly if there are unresolved bad feelings between a divorced couple. This parent can exercise incredible influence over his or her children and cause them to be incapable of making a meaningful relationship with their other parent's new mate. Not that the children couldn't, but it is more trouble than it is worth if their parent is going to harass them.

I feel fortunate that my husband's ex-wife and I can be friendly. My love and concern for her children creates a bond between us. On several occasions we have talked over the phone about a problem or the solution to a problem, which has helped one of her children. She is an ex-wife, not an ex-parent.

10. Compound rejection. Because parent-child relationships existed before the new marriage, spouses can feel rejected by being left out of decisions, conversations, and problems.

"One of our out-of-the-nest children came home to live

with us and get on his feet financially," Ann said. "It worked fine until he began to have trouble. It seemed like I was set outside of things that were going on in his life."

Ann said there were times when she felt like the visitor and that the home belonged to her husband and his son. It helped to talk through her feelings with both of them and to let them both know that she, too, was concerned about his problems and their resolution.

Dorothy told that she found herself being overtly attacked in her own home. Each morning her husband's son would come to work in a family business.

"He would come in for coffee," she said. "I found myself too often on the receiving end of ridicule by this young man. He poked fun at my hobbies and my faith."

Many mornings Dorothy was reduced to tears. She shared her hurt with her husband and asked him to speak to his son about the ridicule. Her husband, however, pointed out that, because his son had never witnessed a healthy relationship between a man and a woman, he hoped they could model a relationship that his son would see as different and good.

Dorothy felt doubly rejected.

"I am astonished by the cold antagonism I feel from my husband's children," she said. "Sometimes I feel totally shut out by my husband and his children. I realize they shared a common past which did not include me. But knowing it doesn't take away the hurt."

Stepparents and adult stepchildren are both on the receiving end of rejection. Children reject stepparents. Stepparents reject children. The children reject one another. Sometimes when families get embroiled in the fighting between the new mate and/or the children, the men and women in the new marriage will even find themselves rejecting one another.

While being on the receiving end of rejection is painful, it is also unpleasant to watch a child or a stepparent being rejected.

This, too, takes time to deal with and needs the grace of

God in addition to openness and honesty on the part of all family members.

One woman described how sick she felt when her husband responded to her stepfather in a negative and disrespectful way. "I wanted our home to be a safe haven," she said.

When she talked to her husband about his comments and attitude toward her stepfather she related her own pain and asked him, "Do you want to hurt me and my mother, too?"

He did not, and when he saw the results of his behavior he promised that he would make a concerted effort to treat the old man with respect, even if he didn't deserve it.

This woman could have been further disappointed because of what she wanted. Here was an example of expectations that might not have been met.

It hurts to care and yet never get genuine love and loyalty such as a natural parent or child receives. Still, it is poison to compare step relationships with their biological counterparts. Although remarriages have special problems, it is not uncommon for similar problems to occur in intact families. Stepparents and adult stepchildren must find different ways of feeling rewarded.

8

Bonding the Primary Relationship

The great need among remarried couples is spiritual commitment," says David Hocking. "That commitment is to God first, and then to your marital partner, and to your children."[1]

Giving God the place of honor in your remarriage, the unseen guest at every meal, will bring bonding in the husband-wife relationship. God is the author of the marriage covenant. Genesis 2:18, 23–24 says: "The LORD God said, 'It is not good for the man to be alone. I will make a helper suitable for him.' The man said, 'This is now bone of my bones and flesh of my flesh; she shall be called woman, for she was taken out of man.' For this reason a man will leave his father and mother and be united to his wife, and they will become one flesh."

Jesus said in Mark 10:8–9: "So they are no longer two, but one." Then he added, "Therefore, what God has joined together let man not separate."

Could God's concept of the marriage bond be more plainly stated? Nothing and no one should interfere with that most intimate and meaningful of all human relationships.

Forsaking All Others

When young people marry, they have vowed to leave their parents and cleave only to one another. Sometimes that is difficult because of their youth, because of their life-long dependence on parents, and sometimes because of the parents' strong hold on their children. Everyone knows of instances where marriages have been destroyed, or have been kept from being strong, by unhealthy attachments to parents.

But what about midlife marriages? Shouldn't those of us past middle age already be disconnected from our parents? Many of us will not even have living parents. Whom, then, are we to forsake?

When I married Bud, Stephen was twenty-one years old and independent, but Sara at fifteen still needed a close mother-daughter tie. I knew, however, that Bud must become number-one in my life after God. Fortunately I never had to verbally tell my children that they were number two. But if I had, I am sure that God would have given me the words and the grace to make certain they were secure in my love and that I was seeking only to obey God by putting Bud first in my life.

Jerry didn't have it quite so easy. His daughter caused him no small amount of trouble. "She refused to relate to Sharon," he said. "She ignored my wife, rebelled at anything Sharon wanted or wished." He described the change that took place. "One day I came home and sat down at the kitchen table with my daughter. I reassured her of my love for her. Then I told her, 'Sharon is my wife now and she is number-one on my list of priorities. She comes before you do.'" The girl was shocked and surprised, but in only a few days she came to Sharon with an apology for her behavior and said, "If Dad likes you that much, I'm going to learn to like you, too."

That kind of honesty and forthrightness clears the air. There could be no misunderstanding or question about where her father's allegiance was. His new wife surely felt affirmed and loved because of his stand.

Are there other people or things you need to forsake to put your husband or wife into the proper position in your remarriage? Have you, for example, forsaken the attractive secretary with whom you flirt during coffee breaks? How about that special someone, male or female, who has been the recipient of your intimate thoughts in conversation? Or how about all of those hours you spend late at the office working? Or bowling with the guys or gals? Or at ballgames?

Many remarried couples think they will take care of their children, their parents, their work, getting their new home shipshape, and every other issue that arises, and when everything else is taken care of, *then* they will think about their marriage and themselves.

Do that and you'll watch another marriage go down the tubes. Every problem will never be solved. Remarried couples have to pool their resources and keep outsiders far enough away so they can establish themselves as a couple first.

Set New Rules

Things will change for you and your family when you remarry. There may be a need to establish new rules for your children, your parents, maybe even your friends.

Have you, during your years as a single, developed habits or traditions that need to be rethought? Changed? Have your parents come religiously every Sunday evening to eat with you? Or have you gone to their house every week after church for Mom's Sunday dinner? Have your children made your home an easily accessible and cheap motel on weekends?

One couple married, and for the first two years of their marriage the groom's best friend came every weekend to eat and sleep over. The bride was understandably discouraged, because she and her husband never had a weekend to themselves. Her husband, on the other hand, seemed unconcerned, comfortable with his old patterns and his old friend.

Two weekends would have been enough for me! I would have sat down with my husband and asked him to establish some new rules. Perhaps the husband needed to forsake this friend and put his wife in first place in their marriage. Why did she put up with that kind of intrusion on their privacy and marriage for so long?

Why are we sometimes slow to make our wishes known? Do we fear rejection or anger from our family or friends if we change the rules or make decisions that will enrich our marriage? What have we got to lose? We can either let thoughtless people set the tone for our marriage, or we can take the responsibility.

Discuss these things with your intended spouse now. Ask good questions. What activities do you do on a regular schedule? Whom do you visit regularly? Is there a pattern to the way someone visits you? Do you do something on a weekly basis that I should know about? Determine together which things you will continue, which you will do together, and which visits or visitors you will sacrifice.

As you decide whether or not to live in your home or that of your spouse, or whether to buy a new home together, now is the time to let your children, parents, and any other friends know what your new rules will be.

Respect and consideration dictate that family members call first to see if it is convenient for them to come for the weekend, to sleep over, to come for dinner, whatever the case may be. And this thoughtfulness goes the other way, too. You and your spouse should never drop in on your family without first calling.

Make Love a Priority

Learning to love God's way will help you get a foundation for your remarriage that will make it successful. God's kind of love is made clear in 1 Corinthians 13:4–7:

Love is patient, love is kind. It does not envy, it does not boast, it is not proud. It is not rude, it is not self-seeking, it is not easily angered, it keeps no record of wrongs. Love does not delight in evil but rejoices with the truth. It always protects, always trusts, always hopes, always perseveres.

In my Bible I have written above this passage *Insert Helen for love*. When I need to reread these verses and be reminded of God's kind of love, it will say, "Helen is patient, Helen is kind, etc." While there is often a sharp sting of conviction, reading this with my name in it makes me accountable to God and shows me how far I have fallen short of his kind of love.

"How Love Came Back," a *Guideposts* magazine article, expresses God's kind of love. A husband was driving to be with his family at their beach cottage. He had heard something on the radio that made him promise to try to be a loving husband and father for the whole two weeks, no ifs, ands, or buts.

"I had to admit that I had been a selfish husband—that our love had been dulled by my own insensitivity," he said. He enumerated several ways: chiding his wife for tardiness, insisting on the TV channel *he* wanted to watch, throwing out newspapers he knew his wife hadn't had a chance to read.

He put his vow to work from the moment he walked into the cottage and kissed his wife. When she suggested a walk on the beach, instead of sitting and reading, he went. He did not call his office, he did visit a museum, he held his tongue when his wife made them late for a dinner party.

The radio commentator had said, "Love is an act of [the] will. A person can *choose* to love."[2] And he had chosen the better way.

What does this kind of love entail for the long haul?

Communicating Love

Most men and women desire that their remarriage be better than the previous one. They want to build a new life.

Communicating love is one of the most important keys to bonding that new midlife marriage. I love to say "I love you" to my husband. I also like to hear it said to me. But I always have to guard against thinking that the purpose of life is to bring delight to *me*. Love thinks of others first.

From a woman's point of view (tested for accuracy on my husband) here are just a few suggestions for communicating love to your mate if you remarry. All of them fit within the 1 Corinthians 13 kind of love. I'm sure you will think of other ways, too.

1. Communicate with compliments. Swap compliments freely and sincerely. Compliments are signs of admiration and praise. When given with respect and honesty they are encouraging.

I once took a Bible class titled "You Can be the Wife of a Happy Husband." Actually I took it twice. I like to say I have a "Ph.D. in happy husbands." The leader of the group admonished us to find something to compliment our husbands for each day. One woman said the only thing she could find good about her husband was that he smelled good. So she told him that every day. Even that insignificant compliment encouraged her in a lackluster marriage, and before too many days had passed she had found other things that she genuinely liked about her husband. Kind words of praise insure that your mate is not being taken for granted.

Public affirmation makes one feel special. There have been a number of times in our marriage when someone has told me something kind or praiseworthy that my husband said about me. What a warm fuzzy it was! It is also nice to make loving comments publicly in a mate's presence.

Marriages in which honest communication has broken down will find one person lobbing small insults in the presence of others. She may have a smile on her face, but it's a picky little dig meant to hurt. Public criticism does not show honor or love. Never do it.

"Reckless words pierce like a sword, but the tongue of the wise brings healing" (Prov. 12:18).

2. Communicate with affection. I hope it goes without saying that affection—both the giving and receiving of it—is a necessary ingredient in a loving relationship.

Many books have been written on sexual love and intimacy. Many of them confirm that a hug or a kiss or a special look across the room does not necessarily lead to the bedroom, although it might. The point is (I'll go ahead and make it again) that both men and women, but women especially, need to know they are cared for and loved through simple affection, the kind that *does not* lead to a romp in the feathers. Many women lament that they never receive affection unless their husbands want to make love. Is that just the way men are? Or has someone given them inaccurate and incomplete information? The power of regular hugs and warm affection should never be underestimated.

Men, if it is your plan to have the hug or kiss lead to the bedroom later, here's a piece of informational trivia which may help you. Though many of you will never have held an iron in your hands, you know what an iron is. When plugged in it slowly heats up. That's the way women are, too. It takes a while to heat them up, and then they take a while to cool down.

Daily doses of simple affection—holding hands, a kiss on the neck, a warm hug, a wink, a scratch on the back—are all needed warmup exercises whether or not sexual intercourse is the culmination.

3. Communicate acceptance. Accept your partner—warts and all. "You can accept and adjust to your partner without *condoning* everything he or she does," says Ken Abraham, "but you can also learn to accept and adjust without *condemning*."[3]

Opposites attract. It's true. Bud and I are as different as day and night. Early in our marriage he called me a "finely tuned race horse." And he acknowledged his own status as a "plodder." After ten years of marriage, I have slowed down; Bud may have sped up in certain areas (though I can't think of any right now). We have accepted one another. Our gait is more nearly the same speed. And, as is God's plan, I believe, we have complemented one another's strengths.

In the first months of our marriage I wondered if I had

any worth at all. Having been a busy career woman with an advertising staff of thirty-five, I was now Bud Hunter's wife. That's it. I no longer received a weekly piece of paper that could be traded for money and which proved my value. Bud accepted me during that transition time. I was worthy of his provision; my heart knew it. But my head kept telling me, "Get a job." It was difficult to make the change to marriage and unemployment.

You and your new spouse will make monumental changes, too. It will be helpful if you both practice acceptance. Do not allow yourself to find fault. "Nothing heals if you pick it," is a saying I heard frequently as a child. It still works.

Reassurance of your love and acceptance of your mate is a godly attribute. "Accept one another, then, just as Christ accepted you, in order to bring praise to God" (Rom. 15:7).

4. *Communicate by listening.* More than half of all your communication takes place without you ever opening your mouth.

Communication breaks down when you know the other person is not listening. Too many of us (I include myself) are busy preparing our answers, even before our spouses have finished speaking. That's rude, and Scripture says love is not rude.

Wilma, a friend of mine in Florida, tells of the time she ran one line in the classified ads: "Will listen" and her phone number. The response was incredible. Hundreds of people wanted to talk and have someone listen.

Proverbs 1:5 says, "Let the wise listen and add to their learning."

5. *Communicate truth.* "Our personal security is based on the assumption that those we love will be honest with us," says Leo Buscaglia, the world's guru of love. "Trust is impossible without truth. And when there is no truth there can be no love."[4]

Most everyone has told a lie at one time or another. Even children know that telling a lie does not bring freedom. Instead, it brings bondage—slavery to sin. To keep sin from being known another lie must be told, and another lie, and another.

Openness and honesty are musts in any marriage. Don't hide things from your mate. Don't tell lies. Lying is betrayal of trust. Where there is falsehood there is no room for trust.

"Whoever of you loves life and desires to see many good days, keep your tongue from evil and your lips from speaking lies" (Ps. 34:12, 13).

6. *Communicate freedom.* One woman revealed that her second husband was so jealous she felt she could not move without his suspecting her of unfaithfulness or dishonesty. She had done nothing to cause his mistrust of her. He had a jealous streak, a carryover from his previous marriage. He was destroying their marriage with his accusations, holding his wife a prisoner.

It is not reasonable to expect a mate to be responsible for your emotional needs or happiness. That's a heavy burden! At the same time, you can never possess someone else. Loving a mate means giving him or her space and the freedom to be who God created him or her to be.

7. *Communicate patience.* "Marital happiness is not automatic, even when both partners love the Lord," says Ken Abraham. "It takes time to adjust to each other, to get used to doing things in new ways, to adapt, and to establish some sensible and satisfactory systems for living together as husband and wife."[5]

There will be many areas in your new marriage where patience will save the day. "A patient man [or woman] has great understanding, but a quick-tempered man displays folly" (Prov. 14:29).

Many of us at middle age and older have habits and methods for doing things that have been ingrained for many years. Maybe some of them are carryovers from a previous marriage. Some habits became part of our lives when we were single and responsible only to ourselves.

My kitchen became a haven during the first months of our marriage, a place where I could feel secure. What I did there would probably help to cement our marriage bonds.

But the kitchen had been Bud's before I moved into his house. He had his ways of doing things. He kept lots of things out on his counters. I put lots of things away. It took patience on both of our parts to learn about each other's home-management styles. He used lots of paper plates and cups. Along came Helen with two sets of pottery and two sets of fine china and all the silver and crystal accoutrements for fine dining. Bud did not think it was all necessary. I did. Patience.

In all of these examples of communicating love, you will get back what you give. Sow love, harvest love; love will bond your marriage. Sow discontent, harvest discontent; your marriage will not survive. It's up to you.

9

Handling Hurts

He drew a circle that shut me out,
Heretic, rebel, a thing to flout.
But love and I had the wit to win;
We drew a circle that took him in.

Edwin Markham

Early in my remarriage I felt helpless. Shut out. I was vulnerable. I wanted to run, hide.

"We rarely take a hard look at the commitment to self-protection that displays itself most clearly in our ways of relating to people. If the core business of life is to love each other as God loves us, then a priority effort to play it safe interferes with the purpose of living," writes Christian counselor Larry Crabb.

Experiencing pain can either drive us closer to God or it can help us to rationalize adding one more brick to the wall of self-protection that we so capably put around ourselves to keep the hurt out.

People in remarriage are familiar with pain in relationship issues both from stepfamily members and sometimes from mates. Often the negative energy spent on peripheral relationships saps the strength from a marriage.

From the vantage point of ten years in a remarriage, and the 20-20 vision that accompanies hindsight, I can view the early relational problems in our marriage with a more rational mind.

Now I believe that most of the hurts I experienced fell into three categories: real, imagined, and set up.

Let's deal with them in reverse order. As I promised in chapter 7, these ideas are sure to help you handle the hurts.

Set-up Hurts

There is no greater way to get into a vulnerable situation and set yourself up for hurts than to expect someone to respond or behave in a certain way. Disappointments are the harvest of unreasonable expectations. Every time.

As you prepare for remarriage do you have the picture of "one big happy family" in your mind's eye? Probably your expectations are too high, at least initially. If the remarriage and family relationships don't turn out according to your plan, bitterness, jealousy, and guilt are liable to be the outcomes.

Lower your expectations. Better yet, get rid of them altogether. Be patient. As I said earlier in this book, it usually takes nearly seven or eight years for things to iron out in a stepfamily. But what if they never do?

Accept the reality of your situation. You are about to become involved with people—unrelated to you in the true sense of the word—who have different values, behaviors, lifestyles, even if they are Christians.

"Every person in my life lets me down, as I let down every person in my life," wrote Traci Mullins. "Awareness of this reality could discourage me to the point of cynicism: Why bother with close relationships if their ultimate end is only disappointment? Because God says life is to be found in losing it, that saving our lives by shielding ourselves from disappointment ultimately leads to ever greater loss."[2]

The essence of life is relational—with God and his family as well as with the family he has given you. Develop a tough skin. Keep the little things little things. If you dwell on a little thing too long, it will become much bigger in your mind.

Which leads me to imagined hurts.

Imagined Hurts

Offense is taken where no offense was intended. Can you remember from childhood when your best friend was acting "mad," and you played guessing games: "Was it something I said? What did I do?" The friend was often too unreasonable to tell you.

We are grown up now. Unfortunately, similar offenses pop up in our adult relationships, too. Paranoia visits. We go through stages of feeling superior then inferior, both rooted in self-centeredness. Some people, for reasons I'll never understand, look for things for which to be responsible. That's crazy behavior. You need not take all the credit nor the blame for every problem.

Author-pastor-teacher David Hocking points a finger at a "wrong standard of evaluating each other." He says that our feelings become the basis for our responses. "I feel" is not always based in fact. One woman in a short counseling session with Hocking used the words *I feel* over twenty times. When he called it to her attention, she admitted that though she did not have any facts, this was the way she felt about her husband. Her feelings were controlling her responses. Her feelings made more of the situation than the facts warranted.

There may be times you will have to deal with hurtful responses and actions directed toward you in your marriage, perhaps from your spouse or another member of your new family. Try to remember that some of the actions and responses will not be about you or anything that you have said or done. Often responses come from whatever is going on within the other person.

Real Hurts

Real hurts are often unmerited. These are the ones you deal with.

There are a number of choices from the world's point of view you can use when real hurts bombard you. You can cope by withdrawing from the hurt or projecting a wall of superiority. Or you can retaliate by attacking with cutting remarks, criticism, sarcasm. Laughing it off, pretending it doesn't matter, doesn't hurt, is a choice that denies reality.

One counselor describes holding on to hurts as the "emotional trading stamp syndrome." You save up every irritation in your memory book, then when you've collected enough stamps, you cash in the books in an explosion of anger.

All of the above are normal "fleshly" reactions to hurt. Obviously, none of them are valid ways for a mature person, especially a Christian, to handle hurt. Instead we need to detach the hurt and determine to love. Face and forgive.

The best thing to do is pray. Simplistic? Sometimes the simple answers are the least obvious. James 5:13 says: "Is any one of you in trouble? He should pray." 1 Peter 5:7 says: "Cast all your anxiety on him because he cares for you." I believe Scripture is speaking of emotionally upset or hurting people.

Through prayer, spending time reading Scripture, and reading other books, I determined to allow God to work forgiveness in my heart and at the same time teach me. I tried to keep my focus on the Lord and on the truth that he delights to do the impossible. I gave up my expectations, but not my hope. "And hope does not disappoint us, because God has poured out his love into our hearts by the Holy Spirit, whom he has given us" (Rom. 5:5).

Being still and trusting the Lord to work are hard tasks for men and women who like action and quick resolutions to problems. God sometimes allows these hurts in our lives as means to nudge us toward others who hurt. His whole plan for us involves reaching out with love.

When I felt myself clamming up in particular situations and feeling threatened, I reminded myself that God has given me a friendly and outgoing personality. I tried to view myself realistically. Every response to me is not always about what I have said or done. I frequently said one of my favorite self-counseling lines: "It's not about me." It is just possible that the hurtful actions come out of the other person's own hurt, rejection, or even ignorance.

How does one cope with hurt in situations where healing does not come quickly? "In the light of eternity, unjust rejections of this short lifetime can be translated into avenues for knowing God more deeply and more perceptively," said Elizabeth Skoglund, "and understanding our fellow man with greater perception."[3]

Learn to detach. This simply means loving the person but not letting the behavior (sin?) hook you into responding in unhealthy ways.

One woman described the clear Plexiglas shield she mentally places around her, invisible to both parties, but impenetrable. Hurtful words and actions cannot get through. By her not responding, the power to hurt is defused.

"I learned to detach," said Carla. "It didn't mean I didn't love my stepdaughter. I continued to pray for her and hope for a meaningful relationship. What it meant was that I could no longer make that relationship the focus of my life at the expense of my own mental health and the relationships that I could build with other family members."

One woman described a different anguish. Her new husband did not like her daughter. He did not want her around. When at sixteen she became pregnant, he vowed that neither the girl nor her baby would *ever* come into his house again. The woman is still dealing with bitterness and anger. When her husband says "I don't like your daughter," she hears "I don't like you," because the child is so much a part of her.

Hurts like this strike us when we are least prepared. Sometimes we are tempted to withdraw a measure of affection or concern for the other person. Or we are tempted to lash back with unkind words. Even when we can exercise verbal restraint, we are left with the gaping wound on the inside.

Perhaps not trying so hard is good advice. Sometimes we try too hard to be accepted. We try to please everyone. The effort is not only futile, but we end up hating and rejecting ourselves because we have not done what we really want to do nor been true to what we really believe.

"So what do I do?" you may be asking. In stepfamily relationships the desire for a happy family seems to be a higher priority than with intact families where love and acceptance are taken for granted. Honesty and openness is the best policy. But peace-loving people find it difficult to confront adults' bad behavior. It seems easier to turn the head, cover up.

Denise, a middle-aged stepdaughter, explained how she confronted her stepfather one day when he was yelling at her and her mother. "I just said, 'Stop it. I am not afraid of you. I will not be terrorized by you,'" said Denise. "He was stunned that I spoke up to him. But he quieted down."

Disruptions cannot be allowed. You may need a sit-down confrontation. It should be staged with love and respect; at the same time make clear that you will no longer tolerate or accept the anger or the defensiveness or whatever the destructive behavior is that has been directed toward you.

It is okay to express yourself. There is nothing in the marriage contract that says you should be willing to be treated with disrespect by anyone in your new family. What is the worst thing that can happen if you reject the disrespect?

Many of you will answer, "The worst thing is that there won't be a relationship." I don't think so. You already have a poor or little relationship. The worst thing is that it would stay the same: disrespectful.

The Outrageous Act of Forgiveness

"Forgiveness is the fragrance of the violet which still clings fast to the heel that crushed it," wrote George Roemisch.

As with God's love, we have a model of forgiveness: not our feelings, but the example of Jesus Christ. "Be kind and compassionate to one another, forgiving each other, just as in Christ God forgave you" (Eph. 4:32).

No one can ever force us or trick us into forgiving. It is a totally free act, but an outrageous act—a voluntary forfeit of our right to fairness and to extract sweet revenge. Forgiveness heals. Doesn't it help to forgive others' wrong or bad actions toward us if we can see them as weak and imperfect human beings just like ourselves?

"The only way to heal the pain that will not heal itself is to forgive the person who hurt you," writes author Lewis Smedes. "Forgiving stops the reruns of pain."[4]

Smedes distinguishes forgiving from excusing, from mere acceptance, from tolerating the intolerable; there are times to prosecute even after granting forgiveness.

Forgiveness is not forgetting, either. If you can forget, the offense is probably too small for the serious work of forgiveness. Instead, Smedes calls forgiveness "redemptive remembering." He identifies the following four steps in the process: (1) Hurt. When hurt, true forgivers admit that they suffer. They acknowledge that the wrong done to them matters. (2) Hate. "Hate," Smedes says, "can keep us going while we feel battered, but . . . then hate turns its power against the hater. It saps the energy of the soul, leaving it weaker than before, too weak to create a better life beyond the pain."[5] (3) Healing. "When you forgive someone for hurting you, you perform spiritual surgery inside the soul; you cut away the wrong that was done to you. . . . "[6] (4) Coming together. You open the door to reconciliation with the person doing the hurting. If he or she comes honestly, love can move you toward a new relationship. A person can work numbers one through three by himself. It takes cooperation from the offender to work number four. But healing can begin in any case.

God's love is the reason Christians can glory in tribulation. Anthony Campolo, sociology professor and Christian author-speaker, related the story of a boy who suffered from spastic paralysis. During his time at a Christian camp he was the recipient of heartless treatment from the other boys. They mimicked him. They ridiculed him. One night they chose him to lead the devotions—another effort to have "fun" at his expense.

The boy stood up and in his strained, slurred speech said simply, "Jesus loves me, and I love Jesus!" That was all. Many of the boys began to cry, and revival gripped the camp.

This young lad demonstrated what happens when divine love fills our hearts. It sustains us through bitter rejection and holds us steady in life's fierce storms. It assures us that our hope in Christ will not be disappointed.

In addition to forgiveness, all of the ways of communicating love that were given in chapter 8 will benefit your new relationships with parents and stepchildren (with the possible exception of "Communicate with Affection," simply because of the touching required). Compliments, acceptance, listening, truthfulness, freedom, and patience—if you practice all of those loving and considerate behaviors, I can virtually guarantee you will have a new family falling at your feet.

Finally, build a strong relationship with God. Ask him to fill in the missing pieces for you. He knows more about your hurts than you do. Develop prayer support with other believers and with your pastor. Allow other people to share your burden. "Carry each other's burdens, and in this way you will fulfill the law of Christ" (Gal. 6:2).

10

Holidays: Rest or Ruin?

Ask me what kind of picture I see when I think of Christmas, I'll tell you a Norman Rockwell painting of apple-cheeked children, happy families gathered around a Christmas tree, tables laden with yummy foods, and outside a light snow falling and neighbors singing carols: an all around feeling of good will.

Is that what holidays are like in remarried families? Not usually. But then are holidays like that for traditional families? Birthdays and holidays in every kind of family are an opportunity for either enrichment or conflict.

Life does not echo Rockwell, and any expectations toward that end are usually self-defeating. Letting go of these unrealistic ideas allows our families to be as they are rather than as we would like them to be.

One psychiatrist expressed it like this:

Any celebration that sets up such unrealistic, magical expectations is very unfair to human beings. People are pushed to deny the reality of their own lives—their financial situation,

133

their true relationships. . . . The rest of the year, we talk about being open and honest with each other, but for a couple of weeks we're supposed . . . to pretend that we love everyone, that we're financially able to do things we know we can't do, that we have a great relationship with the kids.[1]

Traditions New and Old

Tevye in *Fiddler on the Roof* fiercely protected TRADITION for tradition's sake.

I agree with Tevye. Tradition is important, particularly in a society that tends to devalue family and consider family gatherings as romantic nonsense.

At the heart of family celebrations are events that could focus on our Christian heritage. Instead, "the significance of these holidays is all but lost in our secularized society," writes Ann Hibbard. "Baby Jesus has been usurped by a secular Santa, the risen Lord has been pushed aside by the Easter bunny, and Thanksgiving is explained as a celebration of friendship with the Indians."[2]

Nevertheless, we need celebrations to bind us to one another. We need to reclaim our spiritual heritage. We need rituals and excuses to gather. We need reasons for our children and grandchildren to say, "Our family always. . . . " That gives a sense of security. But because our lives are constantly being challenged by change, perhaps our traditions should be also.

But whose traditions? In a remarriage two sets have already been established and now thrust together. One family celebrates by throwing big bashes, the other by quiet family dinners. One opens Christmas gifts on Christmas Eve, the other on Christmas morning. How do you choose what to do? Whose tradition gets left out? How do you combine them?

Good traditions get heartily endorsed by everyone involved. A bad tradition is viewed with disdain or at best, ambivalence. At remarriage a new family is created. New traditions are established, old ones blended together.

When Bud and I married, he had a tradition of staying at the cottage after the duck hunting season closed on Thanksgiving Day and preparing a turkey. If his sons hunted with him, they stayed. Sometimes other hunters would stay for dinner; other times he was alone, because many of his hunting buddies had families to go home to. We talked about continuing that tradition after our marriage, but because of family members who visited from out of state, and elderly parents traditionally invited, the distance and accommodations prohibited it.

My children and I had traditions for every major holiday, several of them involving the preparation of special foods. So the first year of my remarriage our traditions were the ones used. Though there were other grown children to consider whose traditions had not been just like ours, it went okay. Since then changes have been made that make our holiday celebrations more accommodating to everyone involved.

One Christmas Eve tradition that came from my family of origin was to serve oyster stew and chili for an early Christmas Eve supper. Somewhere along the way I dispensed with the oyster stew since none of us liked oysters, but a pot of chili could always be found simmering on my stove on Christmas Eve day.

In about our third year of marriage several family members revealed that chili was not their favorite dish. I reasoned that the next year we would either not have chili or we would also have another kind of soup or stew that they would like. Simple? Yes, and it did not ruin Christmas Eve. The tradition is still intact, but other families and other tastes have been drawn into the circle. Some remarried families will find their Christmas and other holiday traditions completely compatible and will blend their ideas without problem.

One family ended up with a new tradition out of necessity when they fed pancakes to her four and his three for breakfast one morning. Now it's a Saturday breakfast tradition.

Julie and David, a remarried family with older teens,

began the tradition of having one empty seat at their dining room table. They went so far as to put a pair of sandals on the floor at that chair. Jesus was the unseen guest at their special meals.

When I remarried I had boxes of decorations for different holidays that my children and I had collected over the years. Since Bud was not big on trimming his home for the holidays, again, our family's traditional trimming for the home was used. Ever since my children were very small, each of them received a special Christmas tree ornament on the evening that we trimmed the tree. I still give them an ornament, even though they are old enough to have their own trees. Now I have given Bud ten special ornaments (most of them with a hunting or fishing theme) and have begun ornament collections for both of our grandchildren. Megan gets an angel each year, Jacob a toy soldier.

When the big holidays rolled around I saw each of them as the time to get out all the fine china and crystal, to polish the sterling and turn our dining room table into a *House Beautiful* show piece. The down side is that, sometimes with help, sometimes without, all the fine things had to be hand washed while the dishwasher sat empty.

"Why don't you make it easy on yourself," Bud said one Christmas season, "and use dishes that you can put in the dishwasher?" I did. And I still set a beautiful table, with the bonus of more time to sit and talk with the family. Another tradition compromise that worked. Now I use the fine china for smaller dinner parties, and it doesn't take all night to get the dishes done.

Gift Giving

Giving gifts is another area where stress is produced. "Giving is not completely altruistic," writes Christian psychologist Gary Collins. "Sometimes gifts are tainted with self-centered motives on the part of the giver. Gifts can be used to manipulate a receiver, making him feel 'bought' or put under obligation."[3]

"A beautiful gift," said the famous Swiss writer Paul Tournier, "enhances the one who gives [but] . . . the gift which is too wonderful does not honor the one who receives; it humiliates him. One which goes beyond ordinary social conventions gives us quickly the feeling of being trapped, of becoming obligated to the giver, especially if we have no means of doing the same for him."[4] Some people are so uncomfortable with giving and receiving gifts they become antisocial.

Sometimes children within traditional families are not happy with what Mom or Dad give them for Christmas. Giving gifts to grown stepchildren and stepparents begs for thoughtfulness and care. At times we can hurt people without really thinking. One divorced husband gave his children a set of drums. They were living with his ex-wife.

Using a familiar old adage about prayer as a springboard, one couple's motto became "The family that *plays* together, stays together." One of their first Christmases as a blended family with nine living children between them, they bought nine bowling balls, each engraved with the child's initials. After having each ball drilled to fit they began to bowl as a family—a tradition with happy memories attached.

Learning about tastes in clothing and home furnishings takes careful observation and keen listening. Starting in late fall and through the Thanksgiving holiday I try to listen carefully to what our children say about things they'd like to have to complement their fall wardrobes or to learn what they are doing in their homes or apartments that might be clues to needed gifts. Sometimes I score a hit when the package is unwrapped. Sometimes I miss, and the gift goes back for exchange.

One year I wrote in a column a suggestion I sincerely believe has merit. I am still winding up my courage to do it in our own family. It had to do with thinking more of others and becoming aware of ways to help the lonely and discouraged. I suggested putting aside the money that you would have spent on each person and giving it to charities of their "choice" in their names. Radical? Perhaps. Even more radical would be matching the money with volunteer time. But think of the joy of hearing what other family members did with the money and their time, of learning how the receivers were blessed by your gift of time and money. It might make the happiest Christmas for everyone concerned.

Going Home Jitters

These suggestions and ideas are not meant to imply that parents and stepparents are the only people who struggle with holidays. Adult children coming home have problems, too. One adult child expressed her feelings of powerlessness when she thought of her mother and the control her mother wielded over her in childhood. She described her fight against becoming childlike again when she prepares to go home. "I really pray," she said, "and ask God to help me remember that I am an adult and do not need to revert to childhood behavior."

Ruth told how once on their way home for a holiday her husband said, "If Mom makes bread pudding, I'm not going to eat it."

"Why, Jerry," she answered, "you like her bread pudding. Why are you saying that?"

"I do not! I have *never* liked bread pudding," Jerry replied. "But she makes me feel guilty if I don't want it, like I'm rejecting her. So I eat it 'cause it's easier."

Each of us should ask ourselves, "What might I be saying or doing that makes our adult children feel uncomfortable when they come home?" Are there statements that "zing" them like a stray bullet? Maybe it's "When are you going to get married?" or "When do you think you'll have another baby?" What food or activity might you be forcing that someone finds intolerable? Is there something that you "always" say to your children that brings a response? We should remember that our grown children are separate from us. Their lives are not our business unless they voluntarily involve us.

Major on the Minors

Perhaps one of the best ways to eliminate the hurts from holidays is to create traditions and customs that are your own. Build on the past.

Talk about the things you used to do when you were kids. Keeping in mind that memories can deceive, think about whether there is something in the past that you would like to resurrect for your new family or for your grandchildren.

Will your family support you in this quest? There may be happy family traditions that they can help recover from the past.

No happy memories in your past? Create a brand new one. Look through magazines that describe families and their holiday traditions. If you see something that appeals to you, borrow it. Give it a try. The idea may become one you'll decide to call your own. Numerous good books that give ideas to make all kinds of family celebrations special are available. (See "Suggestions for Further Reading.")

Get out the old photo albums and revive pleasant memories. Spur storytelling. Show the old 16mm films, or better yet, have them transferred to video as a special gift to your children or stepchildren.

Instead of having your children and your mate's children come during the busy Christmas and Thanksgiving holidays, start a celebration of your own on New Year's Day, or Veteran's Day, or whatever date suits you.

Start "Love Sunday" (maybe in February, traditionally a "love" time of the year) when the whole family is invited, and the decorating theme is hearts and flowers. Let it be known in advance that "love will be spoken" during this time. If you want to have a spiritual emphasis, you may ask in advance that each family member bring something from Scripture—a story that personifies love, a verse that means something special to them—to share with the other guests.

Celebrate events that might not get so much attention. Anniversary dates are special to remember, not only wedding anniversaries but anniversaries of a milestone in someone's life. Maybe someone in your family has achieved five years without smoking or drinking. Celebrate it! Fly a flag with that person's name on it. Remembering the date of your birthday into the Christian family is special. A favorite photo in my album is of friends decorating a cake for me on the event of my tenth year as a Christian.

Celebrating a new job or a special promotion or achievement within your family will bring memories to savor for years to come. Many families use the red "Special Person" plate on these days, making that person's place at the table unique.

Draw the new family into celebrations by asking them to prepare a dish—a favorite pie or salad—and to also bring the recipe. (If that is a burden for them, pies or salads can be purchased.) Showing grown children that they are needed will begin to prepare them for when their children are grown and coming home for the holidays.

Play a board game together as a family. We enjoy Pictionary, Trivial Pursuit, and Scrabble. Another thing we enjoy doing that brings comfortable togetherness is jigsaw puzzles.

Establish a tradition of reading a special story during your holiday event. Since I have been collecting children's Christmas picture books, I'm looking forward to reading them each year to my grandchildren. My daughter and I have begun to talk about what new traditions we will begin now that little grandchildren will be coming home to the grandparents for holidays, such as making ice cream from the snow, helping the little ones to see the awesomeness of God in each snowflake, having an old-fashioned taffy pull, making a gingerbread house, showing little ones how to string popcorn for the birds or make a garland for their Christmas tree. There are so many things that parents and grandparents can do to make holidays and special days happy, memorable times.

Children need the sense of belonging that holiday customs bring. Every year that children participate in important family events they bond with the family, and their sense of pride in their family grows. Often children are the very ones who bring the generations together and renew the family ties.

Holiday Preparation

Talk about holiday events before remarriage. Plan now to have carefree and enjoyable family gatherings, rather than the ruin that some families describe. Give up your expectations about what Christmas or Thanksgiving or birthdays should be.

During high anxiety times, particularly when remarried family members attend different churches or have different beliefs, tensions can be headed off by thoughtful preparation of our hearts and minds. Slow down. Sit still. Don't be in a hurry. Spend time in prayer and meditation. Ask God to reveal how you can be a blessing to someone in your family.

Eliminate what really doesn't need to be done. Don't overextend or overcommit yourself. Most of my busyness at any holiday time is of my own making. No one stands over me demanding cookies or Christmas cards.

Others may struggle with disorganization, procrastination, or poor planning, which crowds out the peace that should be ours no matter what the day or what the event.

Once you are confident your mind and heart are centered on God, don't let anyone ruin your day. Rise above petty disagreements. Refuse to be drawn into dialogue that doesn't bring glory to God. Every holiday—every day of the year—can be a spiritual event.

11

For Richer or Poorer

I wonder how many other couples marry with their home and cars paid for and money in the bank?" my husband asked during our first year of marriage. While we were not rich by the world's standards, nevertheless, our meager holdings had merged nicely to give us security at the beginning of our marriage.

Statistics point to arguments and disagreements about money or the lack of it as one of the major causes for marital breakup. Remarriages are no different. In fact, they can be even more volatile with the multiple obligations and histories involved.

Both partners in the remarriage come with financial histories including not only assets and liabilities, but also money-handling methods. He may save for a rainy day. She may see $1000 as a down payment on a Honda Accord. She may see the use of plastic as a dangerous pastime. He may carry a one-inch collection of credit cards. Both of them will have more years of experience with money than young people who marry. Often there are two incomes but not equal amounts of disposable money. Different numbers

143

of dependents wait in the wings to inherit. There are two sets of debts.

Planned Financial Unity

Complete openness and honesty about assets and liabilities is a must in remarriage. Keeping things from your partner—information about where your money is being spent or how much you have stashed away—will not lead to trust in your relationship. "Nothing is worse than watching two people in their sixties or seventies divorce because they can't work out financial matters," said an attorney specializing in matrimonial law. "It happens all the time though, because the partners were not honest with one another at the time of the marriage."

Some people think their accounts or investments are secret. But if pressed their marriage partners would indicate they "know something." While they may not have the facts, those partners suspect that their mates are doing something secretively and keeping the information from them. It breeds insecurity and eventually marital disharmony. "Secret financial arrangements are damaging to the marital relationship and may cause your partner to have suspicions and doubts as to your loyalty and dependability," writes David Hocking.[1]

Talk over every aspect of spending. Will you put your assets together? If not, who will pay for what? Don't leave these decisions to work themselves out. Don't assume anything.

Jean Lown, an assistant professor at Utah State University, has studied how remarried couples manage their finances. "Overwhelmingly, they follow the model of the nuclear family, merging all their financial assets," she says.[2] It is important, however, to discuss how you will handle assets and whether or not you will put property and other holdings in both marriage partners' names. Though combining assets might lend simplicity and trust-building in the new relationship, it can also work the other way.

Couples have reasons based in their past history for not

wanting to make such a big step immediately. "My first husband wasn't trustworthy. How can I be sure Jim is?" "I want to make sure my wife really loves me before I put my belongings in her name, too." "The house was mine before the remarriage. I don't see why I should put my wife's name on it."

The best advice is that you consult an attorney who can help you answer questions about your financial assets. Couples with children from previous marriages may want to keep separate some or all of the holdings they brought to the marriage. Many people in second marriages use trusts because of their flexibility. A trust allows almost any kind of distribution of your estate and makes it easy to protect your heirs.

What will you do about employment? Many males will want to be the main provider for their family. In midlife, however, there are many circumstances which may make that an impossibility. Bud and I know a number of men who have been offered early retirement as companies prepare to downsize their work force. They find themselves retired before they had planned and sometimes are unable to begin a new career because of their age, or their skills.

In other cases, midlife marriages bring together men and women with disparate ages like the May/December romances we read about. He may be retired and she may decide to continue her career. Or one of the marriage partners may be handicapped or ill and unable to work.

As I mentioned in an earlier chapter, I had been independent and had provided for myself and my children for over ten years before marrying Bud. Initially the thought of quitting my job and giving up the income was difficult because my personal worth was tied to it. When we married, however, we agreed that it would be best for me to be at home and look for part-time assignments to give me fulfillment and any extra income we might need.

One couple described their lives before remarriage. She, the widow of a missionary with four children, had learned to live on limited resources. Her new husband had always had a good salary and lived comfortably, not having to scrimp. In their marriage the amount spent on gifts was a problem to Barbara. It had never occurred to Bob that it was unfair, but whatever his two children asked for he gave them, even if one asked for a $50 item and the other a $200 gift. He was equally generous with her children. But Barbara thought each child should receive a gift of approximately the same amount. They have equalized this during their five-year marriage.

Because many men and women in midlife have lived independently for a number of years, it is common for them after remarrying to make major purchases or incur debts without the awareness or approval of the other partner. That does not make it right, however. To suddenly ask for money or permission to spend it goes against the grain of some people. That is why husbands and wives should discuss their financial matters regularly and agree on major purchases. Discussions about money confirm marital unity.

It is important for both partners in a remarriage to know what their holdings are, what their financial condition is. When I was much younger, I worked in an office and handled the receipts and disbursements for my employer. He received rent payments from properties all over the city in addition to the income from his business. His wife received generous and regular checks, usually without asking. At his death, I was dismayed to discover that his wife had no idea what he owned or what his income was. She had been content to let him handle the financial end of their marriage. Until she could grasp the condition of his estate, she could not go on with her life.

Many husbands handle the money, and wives let them do it, never asking questions or caring to know what their holdings are. It is healthier when husbands and wives both know the status of their financial condition.

In our marriage Bud wants me to handle the bill paying and accounting. He deposits money to my account to take care of them, but he always knows where we stand financially. By the same token, he will frequently set me down and discuss the condition of our holdings so that I am kept up-to-date.

Here are some questions you might want to check out before you tie the knot:

1. Income. If you are both employed, will you put your income together in one account? Can you live on your husband's income? Can you support the new family on your present income, either individual or combined?

"I'm concerned that I can't support you in the manner to which you have become accustomed," Bud said as he looked around my lovely townhome in Minnesota.

"What manner?" I questioned.

"This," he said, waving his hand to encompass the dining room, living room, furniture, draperies, piano, and art.

"Let's take a walk," I said. "See this? It's from a garage sale. I paid a quarter for it. See this grouping of paintings? Two of them are greeting cards which I have matted and framed. See this lovely piece of furniture? I paid $4.00 at an auction." Because Bud was also a scrounger of valuable pieces, it was just another way that our lives melded nicely.

2. Assets. Home, car, boats, furniture, other properties? Bank accounts? Stocks, bonds? Will these be held jointly? Or will they be kept in individual names? Is the former spouse involved in any of them?

3. Insurance policies. Life, health, disability, home owners, automobile, boat, etc. Make an inventory and decide what changes in beneficiary need to be made. Are there policies for your children that are paid up, or of which they should take over ownership?

After we were married we combined our automobile insurance policies to get the best prices. For a while, when some of the kids were still home, it seemed we had fleet insurance. But it did save money to put all of our autos with the same company.

4. Liabilities. What does each of you owe? Include mortgage, car payments, child support, financial obligations to the first wife, and credit cards. Income taxes! Are they paid up to date?

Be sure you know one another's financial obligations. People sometimes have an instant onset of "vague-itis" when it's time to list liabilities. Before remarriage, not after, is the time to come clean about what you owe.

Many couples who have been divorced continue to pay child support until their children are twenty-one years old or have left college. Usually this sum must come right off the top of any income. It can represent a source of bitterness unless it is talked about before remarriage. First-family responsibilities should be taken care of first.

"The prospect of this financial outlay or drain on a new marriage might be expected to discourage remarriage—but it doesn't," writes author Leslie Westoff. "People usually enter second marriages prepared to sacrifice—even willing to dip into savings."[3]

Whatever the financial responsibilities are, couples remarrying should decide in advance whether or not they can handle them and how.

5. Spending habits. How does each of you spend money? Do you keep a budget? What is your charitable giving quotient? How do you support God's work? What do you spend on recreation, entertainment, and clothing?

Most married couples have areas of disagreement where spending is concerned. I probably spend more on frills for our home than Bud thinks is necessary. He spends more on fishing equipment than I understand. Every person has spending foibles. Talk about them.

Prenuptial Agreements

"Financial advisers are nearly unanimous in urging blended families to spell out each spouse's financial responsibilities in a legally binding agreement," wrote Charles E. Cohen in *Money* magazine. "Among the most important matters to resolve: whether to share all childcare costs—including budget-busting college bills; whether to merge assets and liabilities; and how to divvy up your estates.

Exactly what you agree to is a matter of personal choice and financial circumstances."[4]

But sometimes that causes problems and hurt feelings. One woman wrote an advice columnist about her feelings when her fiancé, a professional man with two nearly grown children by his first wife from whom he has been divorced for 10 years, asked her to sign a prenuptial agreement. She was hurt and insulted. She tore it up. What she wanted to know was why, if she wasn't the type of person to take a man to the cleaners if the marriage failed, was such an agreement necessary?

The answer is that prenuptial agreements are not always about trust. This man was trying to be sure that his children by his first marriage were well-provided for. It was good common sense and beneficial for all parties concerned.

Couples interviewed answered on both sides of the issue, but all agreed that with the incidence of divorce increasing during the past twenty years, there may be an increased need for premarital agreements. They serve certain purposes, particularly to protect the interests of children of earlier marriages.

One way a man or woman can show that money is not the motive for the remarriage is by signing the prenuptial agreement. It can always be torn up or changed. It is not made in stone.

Couples marrying and living on fixed or limited incomes would not have the same concerns as those partners who (either or both) have a good deal of money and desire that their children or other heirs receive most of the estate. Also, a monied partner may not desire to have a potentially large estate revert to surviving spouse when a marriage relationship is not of long standing.

A form of prenuptial agreement that often proves satisfying to many persons who marry in their later years is a will provision that establishes a trust (the principal being equivalent to a third or half of the estate) for the surviving spouse, with the income from that trust payable to the survivor during his or her lifetime. Following that person's death, the principal of the trust reverts to whoever was designated in the original will. What does this accomplish? The spouse's needs are met—the husband and wife of one's later years—without also providing money for his or her heirs; that is, it does not enrich the children and grandchildren of the survivor who has been the beneficiary of the trust.[5]

One couple described a sliding scale that they established at remarriage regarding proceeds from his life insurance. It would go into a trust fund which would provide for his wife. If she died in the first year after his death, 90 percent would go to his children, 10 percent to hers, and the percentages changed each year until it was split equally.

Another family with three grown children in one family and four in the other divided their estate into sevenths and seem happy with that distribution. These details must be worked out by the individuals involved.

Premarital agreements can chill romance. And resentment might be a byproduct of a forced signing of a prenuptial agreement, or the wedding might be canceled if one person finds it really abhorrent. One attorney said he had cases where the parties disagreed during negotiations and later postponed their marriage.

Though prenuptials are purely legal and economic in nature, they are an exercise that should at least be discussed before marriage. Most knowledgeable people encourage each party to retain his or her own attorney.

If remarriage in your midlife is something you are seriously considering, and if you have any doubts about the economics of your plan, don't lay your financial business all out on the table until after you have consulted an attorney who knows matrimonial law, especially as it applies to financial arrangements of mature married people.

Children with Money on Their Minds

When a couple remarries, the older they are the more difficult it is for the grown children. Understandably, it seems unfair that a person who has worked and invested all of his or her life should, in the golden years, remarry someone with no fortune and leave a whole estate to the new spouse without consideration for the grown children. Human nature being what it is, there will be hard feelings.

Though children have no "right" to receive anything from their parents and should not count on receiving an inheritance from them, some grown children "pressure their parents into having a premarital agreement drawn up to assure that the new spouse will not get rich from the marriage," says Claire Berman. "Even more important, it guarantees that the children will not be left poor."[6]

Berman described a situation where a woman had worked as a personnel director, and because she supported her children had been unable to save any money. As she prepared to marry Leonard, Leonard's son felt responsible to draw up a prenuptial agreement for his father and the woman. She was to sign away any right to his property, settling for a fixed sum of money at his death.

She wondered what might happen if Leonard became ill and she had to give up her job to care for him. She saw that as her responsibility. But quitting her job would reduce the amount of her pension. How would she live? Who would take care of her? Leonard had not thought about that. Though they ultimately married without the prenuptial agreement, they have not been able to talk about money at all. Besides, there is a decided coolness between her and the stepson.

You probably wonder what kind of a "weenie" Leonard was to have allowed his son to be so bold. I do, too. But it points up the truth that there are grown children who do try to control their parents. And there are parents who let them.

A good friend related from a grown child's point of view that a prenuptial agreement would have saved many hard feelings in her family.

Her father at seventy, having buried two wives, married for the third time. He desired his children to have *his* money and his new wife's children to have *her* money and possessions at his death. Though that was his wish (and probably hers) they did not have a prenuptial agreement drawn up. And though his will left his home and possessions to his children, the state's law awarded the spouse one-third of his estate.

"When she dies will she give my siblings and me any part of her estate," asked Mary, "when she has two sons of her own standing in line to inherit, too?" To Mary, a prenuptial agreement protects a family in keeping precious possessions and heirlooms in the family.

Wills and Estates

Statistics prove that one out of one person dies. Yet thinking about and finalizing a plan for the disposition of property and personal belongings seems too much for many people.

Following are several reasons that may keep men and women from dealing with wills.

1. Making a will acknowledges mortality. Avoiding the thought of death will not keep the Grim Reaper from your door. Some people find talking about wills and estates even more difficult than talking about everyday money matters. One woman said, "I didn't want to think about a will. I guess I imagined that as soon as I signed it, I might die."

2. People procrastinate. They think they have *years* left to live. They say things such as, "My dad lived to be ninety-two. I've got lots of years left"; or "I'm healthy as a horse. No reason to rush into thinking I'm going to die." When King David penned these words, he knew about the shortness of life: "You have made my days a mere handbreadth; . . . each man's life is but a breath" (Ps. 39:5). And James indicated the same thing when he wrote, "What is your life? You are a mist that appears for a little while and then vanishes" (James 4:14). Who knows when the Lord will call each of us home?

3. Nothing to leave in a will. So why bother with the paper work and the expense of hiring a lawyer to draw up the papers? One little old lady believed that her children would amicably split up her meager belongings when she died, so she steadfastly refused to get to her attorney's office and do the paper work.

Then one of her friends died, and she watched the nearly wholesale slaughter of her children of each other. She saw the greed and malice that leaked out when there was money to be had.

She changed her mind and made a will, even though she still felt she didn't have much to give. Only a short time before her death, an uncle died unexpectedly, leaving his entire estate to her. It boosted her estate considerably. She died a very wealthy woman. And because she had a will, her estate went where *she* wanted it rather than being squandered in a mire of legal battles and used in a manner inconsistent with her wishes.

Making a will is one of the most important things you can do for your own peace of mind. Even more, it is one of the most loving things you can do for your family. Too many people still leave the handling of their property, money, and personal belongings to chance (or the state), assuming (there's that word again) that their wishes will be met.

"Especially traumatic is what happens to the widow when a man dies without a will. Most states allow her from one-fifth to one-half of the estate, with the remainder going to the children," says John Watts, director of planned giving for the Navigators. "In some states one child may receive two-thirds of the estate and the widow one-third. In other states aged dependent parents may be unintentionally disinherited. In many states, when a man dies without surviving children the widow will have to share the estate with her husband's parents, brothers, sisters, nephews and nieces."[7]

"The most expensive route to go home to be with the Lord is by way of intestacy (dying without a will)."[8]

"Estate planning poses particularly delicate problems for blended-family parents who want to protect their biological offspring without neglecting or offending their spouse and stepchildren," says Charles Cohen.[9]

How should a couple handle the parceling out of their estate when two unrelated families are involved? The first piece of advice is to consult a qualified attorney. Never, never try to write your own will or trust. Consider it like trying to set your own broken arm. Don't do it.

You can keep a legacy intact by directing a lawyer to draw up a trust naming your children as beneficiaries. On your death the assets which you designate will fund the trust and can be managed by the person of your choice. You can specify the ages at which you wish your children to receive benefits or lump sum payments from the trust.

A husband who desires to provide for his second wife until her death can draw a "bypass" trust, which gives her the benefit of his estate while she is living.

Whom have you made executor of your estate? What are your children expecting when you die? Will there be problems in deciding what is yours? What is mine? And what is ours? Stepchildren don't inherit property from a stepparent as a legal right. Special provisions must be made. And if they are not, any distant blood relative has precedence.

These issues of money and inheritance are another area in midlife remarriage that needs to be discussed thoroughly and planned carefully before the wedding day and then executed legally as soon as possible.

What if I had died in the first year or two of our marriage? Would my husband have taken care of my daughter's financial needs while she was still a minor? Would Steve and Sara have received anything from my estate? What if after ten years of marriage Bud passed on to be with the Lord, and then when I died only my children inherited? We don't think that would be fair. But where is the protection for our families? Let this time of changing be a seal on your remarriage. Change your wills and be sure to include stepchildren.

Then, it is important to keep the will up-to-date with the

changes in your family. Births, deaths, marriages, and divorces are all occasions to think about reviewing your will. If changes are needed, a codicil (an amendment to an existing will) can be made to replace a section that is no longer valid. Again, consult an attorney.

People who have taken the time to plan their estates and write their wills often heave huge sighs of relief when it is over, expressing how peaceful they feel to know that they have planned for their families. God is honored when we prudently plan for our families after our death.

12

In Sickness and in Health

The phone, usually silent at our lake cottage, rang. I hurried in from the lawn to catch it.

"Helen, this is Amy. I'm calling to tell you that Bud won't be coming down this morning."

"Why? What's the matter?" I asked, adrenalin already coursing through my body.

"Bud didn't want me to tell you 'cause he knew you'd worry, but he checked himself into Mercy Hospital this morning, and they have put him in ICU to give him blood transfusions."

"Why?" Again, the spurt of adrenalin. My mind covered several potentialities. Accident? Heart? Even things that do not involve transfusion.

"Apparently his ulcer was bleeding, and he has lost a lot of blood internally."

"I'll come right home," I said.

I remember the feelings of fear as I began the drive home. My mind was whirling with thoughts and prayers for him. Though I knew the road as well as the back of my hand, I was so distracted I forgot which road to turn on.

In our five years of marriage both of us had been healthy. This was my first experience with a serious illness in my marriage.

After Bud had been several days in the hospital and received several blood transfusions, his medication was adjusted, and he came home with instructions to cut back on caffeine and tobacco—both of which he did faithfully, but not without psychological pain. In addition to the withdrawal from caffeine and tobacco, Bud and I both faced our mortality.

The brief illness changed both of our lives. His concern, rightly so, was for his own health and well-being. Mine was also for those things and to encourage and help as much as possible his transition to better health.

But on a deeper level I began to think about our years of marriage, a mere five years. We were still getting acquainted. We were beginning to bond, but it was not yet complete.

Illness Exacts a Price

What does a woman or man do when in the early years of a remarriage an illness strikes that debilitates, that tears down? What if he had had a stroke and was handicapped? How would I care for him? Will he stay in the marriage and care for me if I get sick? All illnesses, no matter their severity or prognosis, take their toll on marriage. And the emotional and mental anguish demands an equally high price from the care-giving spouse.

A spouse who said, "I do, in sickness and in health, till death do us part," may under the stress of an illness think (if not say aloud), I can't, I won't. The idea of becoming a caretaker may be unbearable to some men and women, even those who have been married for forty and fifty years. How might it be if they have only been married a short time?

Marvin had a severe stroke in the twelfth month of his remarriage. "When the doctor told us the prognosis, Elizabeth could not cope with it," said Marvin. "I was completely helpless, and she stood over my bed and said she had not included 'in sickness and in health' in her vows. They divorced after only a year of marriage.

Though Elizabeth and Marvin had known one another for thirty years, there had not been enough time between the death of his wife and his remarriage. He had not fully grieved his wife's death. And Elizabeth? Were her motives in marrying Marvin pure? One wonders, when she so specifically left "sickness and health" out of her marriage vows.

"It was the biggest mistake I made in my life," said Marvin. "I suppose we did not communicate about problems and situations very well."

The majority of young couples who marry in their twenties and even in their thirties do not face the same issues as those of us who marry over forty. Married in their twenties, they have over twenty years together before they may be faced with serious illnesses related to aging. They have had years to learn to communicate with one another, to become one. They have established the roles in their marriage and hopefully will have problem-solving skills in place before facing major illness.

Men and women who marry after forty, fifty, and sixty and become ill themselves or face their spouses' health problems will not have had the length of time to bond, to have the synergism that comes with time together.

Yet many men and women over forty have high blood pressure, heart disease, possibility of stroke, cancer, arthritis, and other health problems. How does one cope in a midlife marriage when a mate gets sick? Diseases like Parkinson's, Alzheimer's, and multiple sclerosis, which strike without any warning, can wreak havoc on a new marriage. No one knows who may be a candidate for one of those diseases. There is no way to plan for it.

Betty told about her father-in-law, who remarried in his seventies. They had been married three months when he suffered a severe heart attack. In this life-and-death situation his new wife did not know where to look for insurance cards and medical information. When the ambulance came, somehow she thought to grab his billfold and give it to the medics, who found what they needed to help him.

Discussing health issues is often as difficult as talking about money and wills, but it would seem to be equally as important for people in middle age and older. Betty's father-in-law and his wife might have been more secure if they had spent some time discussing what to do in the event of a health problem. Where are the insurance cards? Are you allergic to any medications? Who is the doctor who has been treating you? Which hospital would you prefer?

Failure to face the possibility of illness or death will not change reality. Nor will looking at the possibilities and talking about them hasten anyone's death or illness.

What could possibly be the harm in asking questions before remarriage about the general health of your prospective mate? "How's your health?" "What is your cholesterol level?" "Do you exercise?" "How's your diet?" "When did you last have a complete physical?" "How much do you smoke?"

Inez, a woman from South Carolina, related that she remarried when she was fifty years old. In the fourth year of marriage her husband had a severe heart attack. Since then he has had another, which has made him a very sick man.

"I could not have made it for fifteen years in this marriage," said Inez, "without God. I don't know how other people do it."

Personal medical history can be discussed openly between two people who love one another. What medicines is your beloved taking? What dosages per day? What are they for? What surgeries has he or she had? Is there a recurrence rate for the disease? If, for example, cancer has been detected and surgically removed, is the person in remission? How long? Has there been chemotherapy or radiation therapy? What is the doctor's prognosis?

Ask about the *family's* medical history. Is there a history of heart disease in the family? Diabetes? Breast cancer? Is there obesity in the family? Is your husband-to-be shaping up to be just like his father, and you just like your mother?

My husband knew that I suffered from migraine headaches before we married. But he couldn't comprehend the intense pain involved. On two occasions he has had to take me to the hospital for shots to ease the pain and stop the vomiting. He has learned that migraine sufferers do not want to be hovered over. They want quiet and darkness.

If questioning your mate or fiancée about health issues seems too clinical for your romance, try to remember that love overcomes a multitude of problems. This chapter is not meant to scare people or cause them to fear remarriage. Far from it! My hope is that sharing these things will speed the bonding. Most people can deal with almost anything if they know what is going on and can talk it through. The hidden things cannot be dealt with. So these suggestions are meant to encourage you to enter a relationship with eyes wide open before you remarry. You will never have to say, "If only I had known."

Did You Know?

There is no reason for us to be ignorant of the statistics published regularly about our health.

Did you know that life survival chances for unremarried, divorced people are lower than for those who are married?

Did you know that four-fifths of both divorced men and women do remarry? The chances are better for young men and women, but even for those who get divorced between forty and forty-five years of age the chance of remarriage is four-fifths for women and three-fifths for men.[1]

Did you know that heart disease is the number-one concern in our country? American males have a one-fifth chance of a heart attack before age sixty-five, with one-fifteenth of them dying from it. Coronary-artery disease is only one-third as common a cause of death in women as in men.

Did you know that heart disease causes more premature deaths than any other disease, and that factors increasing your chances of developing heart disease have been identified as high blood pressure, smoking, cholesterol, lack of exercise, obesity, alcohol, family history, and stress? If you are male and/or black, your chances increase.

Did you know cholesterol, a buzz word of the 1980s, has Americans concerned because of its relationship to heart disease?

Did you know that high blood pressure, or hypertension, is often referred to as a silent disease, because it has no symptoms until it reaches an advanced state? However, if left untreated, it can lead to stroke, heart attack, or kidney damage.

Did you know that anger and hostility can kill you? That the driving force behind hostility is a mistrust of others? This mistrust triggers a rush of adrenalin and other stress hormones that cause your heart to beat faster and harder. "Hostility and anger . . . not only raise the odds that you will develop coronary-artery disease," reports Dr. Redford Williams, "but it may also increase your risk of suffering other life-threatening illnesses."[2]

Did you know that more than 90 percent of colorectal cancer patients are past forty years of age, and men and women are affected in almost equal numbers?

Did you know (I know you know) the Surgeon General has said that "cigarettes are the most important individual health risk in this country, responsible for more premature death and disability than any other known agent"?

One man watched his vibrant, happy wife erode from a normal one hundred thirty pounds to eighty. He watched her prematurely age from smoking. He cared for her through heart disease, therapy for cancerous tumors, and held her when she died at fifty from lung cancer.

Did you know that although 60,000 Americans between the ages of forty and sixty have Alzheimer's, the majority of its 2.5 million victims are older than sixty-five?

These are but a few of the statistics you can know about health when you are over forty. See your doctor for a physical checkup before you remarry. Ask your fiancée to have a physical, too. Then follow the doctor's suggestions for a healthier middle and old age.

Coping with Illness

Melinda Blau wrote in *McCall's* that there are "more than seven million 'well spouses' in the United States—an estimated 70 percent of whom are women—whose partners are suffering from chronic diseases such as MS, cancer, diabetes, kidney disease, post-polio syndrome, coronary diseases, stroke, arthritis, pulmonary diseases, . . . Parkinson's and Alzheimer's diseases. These men and women can spend as long as thirty years in silent, self-imposed isolation as they helplessly watch their loved ones deteriorate."[3]

For the well spouse, life is a constant struggle against debilitating emotional fears, physical and mental exhaustion, and often the complete loss of financial security. "Not surprisingly," writes Blau, "well spouses frequently develop their own medical problems and other signs of stress overload such as chronic fatigue, headaches, irritability and insomnia."[4]

Perhaps you are already remarried and feeling buried under the responsibilities of caring for your spouse. You may feel you have already lost your life's companion and gained an albatross as you watch the person you loved and married steadily dwindling away. Following are some ideas on how to keep loneliness and despair at bay while you continue to remain sensitive to the needs of your sick spouse.

1. Be thankful for "daily bread." At times like this a narrowing of focus may be the only way to survive. Today is the only day we can deal with. We cannot bring back yesterday, and though we may try to predict tomorrow, only God knows what tomorrow will bring. It is his desire for us that we live just this day fully and in dependence on him.

The Israelites, who wandered forty years in the desert with Moses, were given enough food for one day. If they gathered more manna than they needed, it spoiled. Dwelling on a tomorrow that has not yet arrived "spoils" what we have today. If we can only focus on small, serendipitous surprises that are tucked into each of our days—the early-morning sounds of birds awakening, the setting of the sun, the rising of a full moon, the touch of a friend—we will not be so tempted to focus on what may or may not be around the corner.

Though there are no simple resolutions to the pain of caring for a sick loved one, the simplicity of saying to yourself, "What has to be dealt with today," will bring shape to the twenty-four hours ahead of you.

2. *Trust in God every day to renew your strength and keep fear from your door.* Scripture promises he will. "Do not fear, for I am with you; do not be dismayed, for I am your God. I will strengthen you and help you; I will uphold you with my righteous right hand" (Isa. 41:10).

Spending time daily with God in prayer or reading Scripture is the ideal, but you may find you don't have the time or the strength. One woman found spiritual nourishment and strength by listening to and singing along with tapes of hymns and Bible songs.

3. *Do not worry about your life.* "Worry does not empty tomorrow of its sorrow," noted Dutch saint Corrie ten Boom, "it empties today of its strength." If fear can be personified as a roaring lion, then worry is a skittering mouse. Worry steals joy from little things every day. Leave the "what ifs" with God as quickly as they come into your mind.

"Nothing will happen to me today—nothing good, nothing bad—without passing through my Father's hands," are the words of a Christian song. I often hum the tune when I am tempted to dwell on negative things happening in my life. God is sovereign. He is totally in control.

4. *Pity parties are not on the agenda.* Some people cry, "Why is this happening to me?" when problems enter their lives. You might try asking God, "Why *not* me?" In God's economy nothing is wasted. Every event, every setback, every blessing is carefully used for his purpose. Romans 8:28, probably one of the best-known verses in the Bible, con-

firms it. "And we know that in all things God works for the good of those who love him, who have been called according to his purpose." Trust him to use this setback in your life.

A young friend of mine lives in a marriage that stifles her yet is a good illustration of the working out of Romans 8:28. She "deserves" better, say many of her friends. But she steadfastly perseveres in a much-less-than-perfect marriage, believing that the Lord has taught her what she would not have otherwise learned if she had left her husband when well-meaning friends gave her that advice. She sees personal growth in the midst of the struggles.

5. *Ask for the help and prayers of God's people.* God has included us in a biological family to whom we can usually turn in times of need. He has also given us an extended Christian family through our church. One woman related how heartwarming it is to see the joy and eagerness people have when they help her with household chores or do the simple job of taking her husband to the doctor's office.

During the stress of completing this book manuscript, a friend asked, "What can I do to help you?"

Normally I would have said, "Oh, there is nothing you can do. It will just have to wait until I have time." But instead I said, "My flower beds need weeding. I'm frustrated that I can't get to them." Bless her heart! She came over on two evenings and weeded two big flower beds. My burden was lifted, thanks to one of God's people.

Martyrdom does not become you. Many times a caregiving spouse feels as though he or she is the only one who can meet the needs of a sick spouse. In reality, others can ease the burden by sitting for the afternoon while the primary caregiver gets rejuvenated at lunch with a friend or on a brisk walk alone through the park. Everyone needs an emotional pressure valve. No one can give indefinitely from an empty cup. Plan into your life regular outings that will keep you healthy. You may even want to visit with a counselor to help you deal with your feelings of loneliness and despair.

6. Seek good medical help. Nothing would be worse than a lack of trust in your physician or in the hospital where your spouse is being cared for. If you are not confident your doctor is doing everything possible, or if you would be more comfortable with another opinion, speak out.

Also, be sure that you remain in good physical condition.

"In sickness and in health" undoubtedly turns out to be one of the most difficult of the marriage vows. The perseverance needed to remain true to that vow can come only from God.

A woman was partially paralyzed after an accident. During the time she was in bed and unable to even turn herself over, her husband of thirty-six years proposed to her again.

"I want to spend the rest of my life with you," he said. After nearly a year, when she was able to be up and around in a motorized scooter, they renewed their marriage vows—"in sickness and in health, till death do us part."

The reception was a huge and gala event!

13

Parenting Our Parents

My father died when I was only twenty-six, and while I missed him terribly, the Lord had given me a brand new baby to fill some of the emptiness. I remember, though, the deep sorrow I felt when I was in my midforties and my schoolmate's mother died. "My own mother is in that generation," was my thought, "and our generation is next in line. We will be the older generation. Then we will die." The last barrier was gone. Shortly after that the first of my high school classmates died. My mortality was suddenly in clear focus.

Today my mother and her husband are eighty. They moved nearly a year ago into a housing complex for the elderly where there is more safety and caring people who will come in a moment if one of them falls or needs help in any way. My stepfather does not hear well, has lost nearly all of his vision, and is in the early stages of Alzheimer's disease. It is difficult for Mother to cope with the changes in her husband and consequently in their life. She is not ready, however, to find other care for him. She looks to me for guidance. I'm not at all sure I'm prepared to give it.

Sandwich Generation

Adult children over forty who have aging parents and grown children have become known as the "sandwich generation." We have passed through the aging process that our children are now in—young adult, yuppie, parent—and are on the edge of the land of maturity where our parents live—prime time, golden age, senior citizens.

When you think about it, going through all of these growing up stages has its humorous and frantic points. As high school graduates, still adolescents, we leave home or go to college to achieve independence, however tentative. "We may need you, but we don't want you" might best describe feelings toward parents.

With marriage comes further withdrawal from the parents who nurtured us, forsaking them in lieu of the men or women to whom we have pledged our lives. We have cut the apron strings for good. We love our parents, but ask that they not interfere in our lives.

Children come and draw us back to our parents, who love our children and want to see them and help care for them.

Many children literally "fly the coop" in midyears as career advancement and family moves for positioning prevent being close to parents except by telephone and mail.

Then after many years of this careful withdrawal *from* parents during the early years of marriage and beginning families of our own, we midlifers now find ourselves drawn *to* our aging parents.

It seems as though we have become the parents, they the children. We can never change roles, however. Assuming true role reversal only strips a parent of dignity and honor. Instead, beginning a new relationship with our parents—one of understanding and love—is the goal for this time in our lives. Look at their lives as blueprints for the future that can teach us many lessons as to what to either strive toward or to avoid.

The words of the apostle Paul in Colossians 3:12–15 are applicable during this time in our lives:

> Therefore, as God's chosen people, holy and dearly loved, clothe yourselves with compassion, kindness, humility, gentleness and patience. Bear with each other and forgive whatever grievances you may have against one another. Forgive as the Lord forgave you. And over all these virtues put on love, which binds them all together in perfect unity. Let the peace of Christ rule in your hearts, since as members of one body you were called to peace. And be thankful.

Parents still have their own rights and needs, albeit limitations. How you handle the physical and emotional demands of aging parents or stepparents will give you volumes to think about. Can they care for themselves? Do they have the financial means to continue to live in their home? Could they move in with you? *Should* they move in with you? How will you handle this new role in your remarriage? Will your new spouse support you? What is your responsibility to your parents?

Hasty decisions are not good for your parents and might threaten even the stability of your marriage.

Again, Scripture gives guidance: "Listen to your father, who gave you life, and do not despise your mother when she is old" (Prov. 23:22). From the handing down of the Ten Commandments one thing remains clear: "Honor your father and your mother, so that you may live long in the land the LORD your God is giving you" (Exod. 20:12).

"In the case of an aging parent," writes Amanda Lloyd, "to honor requires us to care, love, sacrifice, and be patient during some of the most trying times in a child-parent relationship."[1] Whatever you do, seek God's guidance and direction in your decisions.

We would not think of going to school, getting married, becoming pregnant, or retiring without planning. Yet we fail to plan for caring for a parent who can no longer care for him or herself. Elaine Cohen recommends that grown children take the step of discussing this subject with their aging parents. She offers the following check list as a starting point for discussing your parent's future:[2]

1. Do your parents have frequent medical and dental checkups?
2. If living alone, does your mother or father know how to prepare easy, inexpensive, nutritious meals?
3. Is your parents' home safe? Are there handrails on stairways and protection against slipping in the bathroom?
4. Whom can your parents call for chores, transportation, and small emergencies?
5. Would moving to an apartment building or senior citizen complex improve your parents' safety and social contacts?
6. Is your parents' home easily accessible to shopping, churches, and recreation?
7. Have you and your parents discussed an action plan if catastrophic illness strikes and they are physically disabled?
8. If they move, would health care be available if they became incapacitated? Would they still be eligible for medical benefits or services?
9. Do you feel a surviving parent should live with you? Does your spouse agree with your feelings? What would be the financial arrangements? Where would the parent's living space be?
10. Have your parents discussed their financial situation with you?
11. Have you and your parents met with an attorney to discuss their financial affairs in case of physical or mental incapacity?
12. Are your parents aware of government supplements such as Social Security, Medicare, and Medicaid? Do they know how to apply?

13. Can your parents afford to pay the bills until Medicare or other reimbursement comes?
14. Do your parents have supplemental health insurance?

Caring for an aging parent does not have to be a harrowing experience if you face the future with a plan and are mentally and emotionally prepared. It is better, too, to plan ahead while a parent is still functioning normally.

Patience, endless patience, is required to care for an elderly person. If you don't have patience, it won't matter what else you have.

"The dictionary defines compassion as 'sorrow for the sufferings of others, accompanied by *an urge to help*,'" writes Shirley Flanagan.[3] She says that elderly people are troubled because of their failing health, particularly if they were once strong; that they are often lonely; and that with compassion we need to take time to sit down and visit.

"If variety is the spice of life, then a good sense of humor is the sugar that keeps it from going sour," Flanagan continues. "When you take on the responsibility of caring for an elderly person, a sense of humor is invaluable in helping you over the "rough spots" along the road you have chosen."[4]

Aging people go through several stages before they become totally dependent. You can recognize these changes: (1) minimal loss as physical strength deteriorates; (2) intermediate stage where the person is partially dependent on self, partially on others; (3) total dependency, cannot function without help.

Financial Considerations

"The longer your parents live, the greater the chance that their financial independence will be destroyed by inflation or the steep costs of a devastating chronic illness. And if that happens, often they can turn only to you for help," writes Eric Schurenberg in *Money* magazine. "The financial choices confronting sandwich families can be the most wrenching any household ever faces. Even if your parents are healthy, you still have to juggle their eventual needs, your responsibility to your children and your own long-term financial goals."[5]

Planning in advance is the only smart thing to do. Review your parents' investments and discover whether or not they are adequately protected against inflation. A fixed retirement income, when placed against a moderate 4.4 percent annual inflation rate, would drop by 50 percent between the ages of sixty-five and eighty-one. What that means is that if the inflation rate remained at 4.4 percent for fifteen years, a $1000 pension would be worth only $500 in purchasing power at the end of the fifteen years. Can your parents live on that?

Other parents may not have any investments and will need help discovering how they will exist. Will their Social Security take care of them? Where will they turn for help if nursing care is needed?

There are so many other considerations, it is mind boggling. Do your parents have long-term care insurance? Many elderly people think that because they are eligible for Medicare they will be taken care of. Unfortunately, Medicare does not cover the most common source of catastrophic expense: chronic disability that requires months, maybe even years, of round-the-clock care.

What do you do then? Will you be able to boost your income to care for your parent(s)? Are there assets your parents can sell to cover some of their increased medical needs? Or are they without assets?

Consult an attorney before your parent(s) go on Medicaid (the medical welfare program). There are assets that are exempt when the government determines the eligibility. But sometimes Medicaid is the only option.

Their Home?

Given a choice and provided they are well enough, most parents prefer to remain in their homes. There may be advantages. Often their home is paid for, or carries a very low interest mortgage.

Your parents are familiar with their surroundings. The neighbors and friends they have come to know and be comfortable with over the years live close by. The church, shopping malls, grocery stores, and even physician may be in the vicinity.

But the time will come when they can no longer remain in familiar surroundings. Then hard decisions have to be made.

Your Home?

Even in traditional families sometimes it isn't always workable for a parent to move into your home. Space may be too limited, both of you may work and not be available to care for a parent, or you may have a family at home whose demands are still great on you.

If it seems workable in your remarried home, could your marriage withstand the pressure? Both the parent and the child must want the arrangement for it to work.

I have heard stories of widowed mothers (or fathers) coming to live with their grown children. The stories would make good fiction plots as the intrigue plays itself out—pitting husband against wife and children against parents. Each of us who are aging should consider how we would want to be if we have to live with one of our children, heaven forbid, and we should also do our best to make an arrangement with one of our parents in our home as peaceful as possible.

One woman sat down and wrote a letter to be opened the day she went to live with one of her children. Some of her thoughts were: to contribute toward her keep; take baths regularly and keep herself neat; remember whose home it is and to be considerate of her child's spouse recognizing that that person made an allowance so she could live with them; make space and privacy for them as much as possible; allow them family vacations by offering to spend a visit with another relative or friend; keep opinions to herself unless asked for them; be open about her plans for burial, hospitalization, and so on.

Wise words from a wise mother.

Transitions

Open communication before, during, and after a move is important for a calm transition and a healthy relationship in the future. There will, however, be sacrifices as well as advantages.

You will sacrifice privacy in your home. Your parents will sacrifice the privacy they have been accustomed to during the years they have lived alone. Both of you will sacrifice space unless your plan is to add on to your home for your parent or make several unused rooms into an apartment for her. A niche of her own is desirable. But will she be able to climb the stairs? Is a bathroom easily accessible? Will she share a bathroom?

There will be added responsibility for you. The parent who has been taking care of himself for years may now be dependent on you for some of his needs. He will sacrifice independence, a painful adjustment for an elderly person who has had unaccustomed limitations on his movement and freedom.

There will be less freedom for you, too, if your parent cannot stay alone. Be prepared to hire someone to come in and give breaks to you and family members.

There will be differences in activities, manners, and values that may cause friction or tension.

An advantage for the parent living with you will be decreased financial outlays, as it will be much less expensive living with you than in a nursing facility or care home. Will your parent share in the household expenses? If so, how will you determine a fair share? If your parent *can* help, accept it graciously. It will make him or her feel more welcome in your home.

Another advantage for you will be the effort saved in visiting them in nursing homes or other care centers. Some of the areas you will want to discuss beforehand and probably many times after the move include the following:

1. Usefulness. Parents like to feel they are part of the household and useful. There will be things they can do in your home that will fill this basic human need, giving them feelings of accomplishment as well as helping you. It may be mending, making household repairs, puttering in the garden, helping with meal preparation or baking, polishing silver, whatever *they* might be interested in doing.

If your parent is a Christian, encourage him or her to pray. Keep prayer needs up-to-date within the family and in the church.

2. Respect. Ask them to respect you as a parent. If you still have children living at home, your parents need to know for sure who gives the children direction. Ask your parents not to interfere in discipline or to overindulge your children.

If they disagree with you, ask them to talk it over in private with you. Listen to them. This way you will fulfill the commandment to "honor your father and mother."

Respect from you and your children is also a must. Children will take the lead from you. If you are respectful and kind, they will be, too. If you are short tempered and say unkind things about their grandparents, your children might have the same attitude.

A grandparent in the home widens children's horizons and often bolsters their faith.

3. Privacy. Discuss entertaining plans in advance. There will be times when you will want to entertain friends apart from a parent. It will work the other way, too. Your parent may want to hostess bridge club and not have you involved. Both parties will need to understand that they are not being rejected when they are not included.

Resentment Buildup

Elderly people are often set in their ways. Trying to change them is as impossible as it is undesirable. Whatever their shortcomings have been, they will be more pronounced with age. Imperfections that were hardly notice-able when they lived in their own home could cause your nerves to jangle.

"Often the responsibility [of caregiving] falls to a woman who has finished raising her own family," says Bette McCaulley. "She's also taking care of one, or sometimes both, of her own or her husband's aging parents."[6]

Whether you are a son or daughter, you may feel trapped by the circumstances, and no answer seems to be the right one. This situation can lead to resentment and bitterness—either against the live-in parent or against the spouse who leaves the house each morning and goes to work, away from the problems within the home. Perhaps other siblings have been unwilling to be involved in the care of their mother or father. You might resent their advice and comments when they have not contributed to helping with their parent.

It is common for parents to speak in glowing terms of their children who are not present. Do not take this as personal criticism nor become defensive and speak harshly to your parent. Resentment will result in bitterness. It will hurt every person involved and ultimately your marriage. If you feel you are carrying an unfair share of the load, set aside time with your mate to talk and pray together.

"No matter how much we try to be loving, forgiving, and guilt-free," writes Marilyn Fanning, "the daily stress of caring for a parent in our home or visiting in a nursing home causes fatigue, irritability, and sometimes depression. These reactions are accentuated by the knowledge that we are perhaps viewing our own future."[7]

Outside Care?

Deciding to put an elderly person in a nursing home is a traumatic decision for all people involved. The emotional and financial drain will be great. Too often the decision is made when someone has been seriously ill for a time, or after a spouse has passed away. Often there has not been time to plan properly.

Nursing homes can be temporary or permanent. There are other options, too. A care home can be matched to a parent's degree of need. There are custodial-care facilities and board-and-care homes, which offer room, board and other helps, and sometimes recreation and transportation.

Grace recently moved into an efficiency apartment in a board-and-care facility. She is able to care for herself, but desired to be situated near home and where others her age live. She is thrilled to have her own furniture arranged attractively in her apartment where she eats breakfast. But she enjoys very much the communal dining room where she can interact with other elderly people during lunch and dinner. She also enjoys the lounges where she can play pinochle and bridge.

I was not aware until recently that nursing home care falls into two categories. Intermediate care facilities (ICFs) care for people who cannot live independently because they are not well enough. Though they do not receive constant medical supervision and nursing, they may need help with bathing, getting dressed, and walking.

Skilled nursing facilities (SNFs) care for people who need constant supervision, skilled nursing care, and rehabilitative therapy. Registered nurses supervise these facilities.

It is wise to do some investigating before making a choice. Following are a few suggestions on things to check:

1. Parent preference. What kind of home is needed for your parent? Is there a recommendation from his or her physician? Does your parent have a preference?
2. Physical condition. Is it well located? Proximity to your parent's friends, family, and doctor should be a consideration. Is it cheerful, clean, and safe?
3. Money matters. What are the costs? How will you finance the care? What is covered under the basic monthly charges? Are there "hidden" costs for services? How are they billed?
4. Tour and inspection. After checking all the possibilities, visit the homes that appealed to you and your

parent. Ask about admission requirements (usually related to money). Ask to meet the administrator or owners of the home. Ask to see the licenses and accreditation. Ask to see a copy of the patients' bill of rights. Is the staff friendly and helpful? Note how they speak to the residents. What activities are available? Stay for lunch. Is the food nutritious and tasty and served in pleasant surroundings? Do they handle special diets?

When you have gathered all the information, you should be able to make a sensible and suitable choice. Lean heavily toward your parent's wishes if possible. With respect, give your parent the right to express his or her own desires. It will ease the transition, no matter what it is.

Guilt—True or False?

There is almost always the danger of guilt clinging to decisions regarding aging parents, of "putting them away."

One fifty-five-year-old woman, divorced and living in a one-bedroom apartment and working full time, had to make a decision regarding her father, who needed full-time care. Her siblings (who lived in another city) thought she should bring their dad to her apartment to live, but Marge felt she should find a nursing home where he would not only have his own room, but would receive the care that she could not provide for him.

One of her brothers thought that was the cruelest decision she could make and proceeded to drizzle guilt all over her. Stories of abuse of the elderly came to her from other families whose parents had gone the nursing home route.

Should Marge have accepted this guilt? When she examined the situation, she could truthfully say she had made the right decision. Her father was comfortable and well cared for. She could visit him and not feel guilty.

This story exemplifies the kinds of feelings involved in making decisions that involve your parents. Guilt feelings are unfounded when children find it impossible, whatever the reason, to care for parents in their home or to have to put them in a nursing facility. We can do only so much and then remember that all of our lives rest in God's hands.

"We can't instantly put away guilt and all the other unwanted negative emotions," says Patricia Rushford. "Those feelings will crop up from time to time like thistles in a garden. We must weed them out, pull them up, and fill their space with good seeds—the positive power of God and prayer."[8]

14

Dream a New Dream

Think romantic. Now is the time to ask your bride-to-be for her hand in marriage. Now is the time to respond with the certainty that you are ready to remarry, "Yes."

At least that is usually how it works.

In our case, when we were gathered with our friends for a picnic supper during a 1979 fishing trip in Minnesota, Bud asked his cousin, Johnny, if he would be the best man in his wedding.

If I had been sharp, I should have asked, "Oh, and who is going to be your bride?" because Bud had not officially asked me to marry him. There were, however, plenty of clues that revealed his intentions. Little things like the long distance phone bills, the increased travel to Minneapolis, not to mention the addition being built on his house.

When he did "officially" ask me, of course I said "yes."

Whether you have been married before and that marriage has been severed through divorce, or whether you have been widowed through the death of your spouse, entering a remarriage is still a "first"—the beginning of a new partnership.

"The poignant symbols of death and resurrection are applicable here," write Myrna and Robert Kysar. "The first marriage is dead, and with it have died the hopes and dreams of the individuals involved. But there may be a resurrection. God brings life out of the death of a marriage. That life may take the form of remarriage."[1]

Dream a new dream!

If you have read through the first thirteen chapters of this book, my fervent hope is that you have carefully considered all of the stumbling blocks that could cause you problems in your remarriage. I hope you have been honest about your feelings and about your prospective spouse's feelings and have spent many hours in discussion about your families, your expectations, your fears, your finances, and your health. Have you prayed individually and together about your decision? And have you trusted God to help you? I pray your love for each other has grown because of talking about the previous chapters in this book. Have the stories of others who have walked down the aisle before you touched your heart? Or brought a smile to your lips? Made you think about yourself? I pray that if you decide to remarry, your new mate will be first, after God, in your heart.

If the two of you have talked through these things, essentially you have planned your marriage.

Now it's time to plan your wedding. Let's face it; any successful activity requires planning—and if you like a party, the exciting and fun part of preparing for remarriage is ahead. Unlike the first marriage, *you* get to make the decisions. Mother and Dad do not dictate guest lists. Probably they won't pay for your wedding, either.

You can throw tradition to the wind. Do exactly what you want to do!

There are lots of things to plan. Let's just walk through them. I'll share some ideas gathered from other midlife remarrieds.

A wedding can be as simple or as spectacular as you want to make it. You may decide to fill the church with friends and relatives. Or you may decide to slip away to the justice of the peace with your witnesses and quietly say "I do." Your wedding can be a simple, low-key, private ceremony, or you may decide to rent a hall and have a grand affair. Let your remarriage say something about who you are as a couple.

The Date, Place, and Time

Clearing a date with the church and the pastor who will marry you is the first hurdle to cross. Many pastors, particularly in evangelical churches, will want to spend time with you in premarital counseling before you say your vows. The trend is for counseling to be taken seriously and for discussions to take place on how relationships succeed and fail.

You might show your pastor *Remarriage in Midlife*. Share what you have learned and how you have come to your decision to remarry to show your pastor that you have given your decision good forethought.

Will you choose to be married in a church? Whose church? Perhaps you both attend the same one. In our case, since Bud was living in Cedar Rapids and I in Minneapolis, we chose to be married in my church—a huge place where our wedding party and guests were dwarfed by the size of the sanctuary. If it had not been under construction, I would have chosen to be married in the Fireside Room, a much smaller and more intimate place where our guests would have been closer and more a part of the ceremony.

Other settings for weddings are also available to you and do not have to detract from the sincerity and meaning of your wedding vows. A backyard or garden wedding during warm-weather months is a beautiful option. Or you may want to solemnize your vows in front of the fireplace in a ski chalet and stay on for your honeymoon.

Friends of ours, each marrying for the second time, married in December in a rustic lodge at one of the county parks. The lodge was trimmed with evergreen and poinsettias. The bride and groom exchanged their vows in the glow of the fireplace. The whole lodge was warm from the fire and the special occasion.

There are as many options available to you as there are ideas. Use your own creativity to make your wedding a memorable event.

When you choose your wedding date allow time ahead for ordering, addressing, and mailing invitations. Or, if you are not going to send invitations, allow time to make calls or send notes to those friends and family you want to attend.

The Invitations

In first weddings the bride usually has the say about most of the plans, with the groom going along. In remarriage that may not be the case.

In divorced families, whether or not to invite former in-laws and ex-spouses to your wedding must be discussed and based strictly on personal ties and feelings. If there is any doubt about someone's comfort at your wedding, or if in fact it might go more smoothly if they didn't come, don't invite.

In our situation, the guest list was one of the first considerations. I would have shared my happiness with everyone—my whole church family (about 1500 people) and all of the people I worked with, my neighbors, and friends. Bud wanted only our immediate families in attendance.

Once again, compromise was the only answer. We invited about fifty people to witness our exchange of vows and about one hundred more to come to a reception in our honor.

Though some etiquette sources say that formal invitations are not usually sent for remarriages, this is only because there are often fewer than fifty guests, so hand-written notes may be sent instead. You may want to experiment by using bright ink colors or having a calligrapher write your invitations for you.

We telephoned our family and friends who would attend the wedding and sent invitations to the reception.

One example of a wedding invitation that had a special message of Christian love was Lenore and Bud's.

In the Presence of God

Lord,
>   my loved one and I,
>   the wedding party,
>   the wedding guests
>   gathered together
>   in the presence of God
>   to unite us
>   as husband and wife
>   in the holy bonds of
>   marriage.

It is an
>   awesome, overwhelming,
>   wonderfully mysterious
>   meaningful experience
>   in our lives.

And Lord,
>   we want to thank you
>   for bringing us together;
>   for our eager hopes
>   and enduring dreams;
>   for our steadfast love
>   and our secure faith.

But Lord,
>   even as the wedding ends
>   and the marriage begins
>   enable us always to live in unity
>   in the presence of God,
>   recognizing you to be
>   the Director of our lives
>   and the Head of our home.

Thank you so very much for coming today and for making this day so special. Our desire is to serve the Lord Jesus Christ and glorify Him in our lives. You each have a very important place in our lives and we will appreciate your prayers and love as we begin our new life together.

In His love,
Bud and Lenore

You may choose instead of a printed invitation to send announcements after your remarriage. If you do, they should be sent within one or two days of the wedding to those people who were not invited. An announcement notifies them of the bride's new name and the couple's new address.

Here is our wedding announcement. After ten years, I still like it very much.

With gratitude to God,
we joyfully announce the
commitment of our lives
to one another
Helen K. White
and C. F. 'Bud' Hunter
Friday, August eighth
Christ Presbyterian Church
Edina, Minnesota
We consider your friendship
and love our treasured
possession and ask that it
be your only gift to us.

Mr. and Mrs. C. F. 'Bud' Hunter
after the eighth of August
1132—21st Street S. E.
Cedar Rapids, Iowa 52403

A published account of your wedding in a local newspaper is another way to tell the news of your betrothal. Check with your newspaper for its regulations regarding submission and publication.

The Flowers and Clothing

As in first weddings, you may decide to wear formal clothing—the bride in a gown and the groom in a tuxedo. The old myth that only a first-time bride may wear white has been replaced with the idea that the wedding itself is symbolized by white rather than the bride's purity. So if you want to wear a white dress, do so. Most of the midlifers I talked to did not choose this route, but opted instead for more simple and less costly attire.

Second-time brides may choose to wear a suit rather than a dress, bright colors rather than the more traditional, off-white, dove gray, or pale mauve. Show ingenuity in putting together a wedding outfit. A bright red suit or dress, softened with white flowers and pearls, might be fun for a holiday wedding. A visit to a vintage second-hand store might net you a Victorian or early-Edwardian dress. Choose your best color and go with it.

I chose a soft grey linen dress with a short jacket trimmed with Cluny lace. My husband-to-be no longer owned a suit, nor did he want to own one, so he wore gray trousers and a navy blazer.

We each had a witness to our vows (the minimum required by law) and their attire was similarly simple.

Marilyn, another midlife bride, opted for a mother-of-the-bride type of dress, a simple brocade with lace in the V neck and on the yoke. She wore baby's breath, dyed to match her dress, in her hair. Marilyn's father and her oldest son escorted her down the aisle.

I chose not to carry flowers; therefore, there was no bouquet to throw and no chance of one of our daughters catching it, thereby disappointing the other. Instead, my attendant and I wore corsages, and Bud and his witness wore boutonnieres. Our parents and our children were the only others who were given flowers to wear.

Involving children from both families can be a distinctive part of a remarriage, a way to include them in an important change in their parents' lives. You may choose not to have your children in the ceremony, but instead ask them to perform one of the many other necessary duties before the wedding or at the reception.

Older remarrieds may choose to have their children stand up with them as witnesses to their vows. That was the case with Verla and Paul, whose nine children all stood up with them in their private wedding ceremony. After the vows were repeated, one of the children said, "Now we're married."

One couple who married in midlife opted for a huge and showy wedding, because neither of their first marriages had been a church wedding. But they sacrificed family attendance. The groom's daughter hoped for a small wedding for her father because she had not finished grieving the loss of her mother. She stayed away. Other family members were confused about just where they should be.

The Wedding

Your wedding ceremony can be very formal, semiformal, or informal. Many remarrieds choose, as we did, to keep the nuptials private and have a larger reception or party afterward.

Nonessential elements of the wedding may be dropped completely or altered to fit the comfort zone of the bride and groom. Some of those elements are the processional, escorting the bride to the altar, and the recessional.

I did not walk down the aisle. Instead both Bud and I waited in a small room just off the front of the church, and when the music ended, we walked out to take our places in front of the pastor. Our witnesses came up from the front pew. As we recessed we paused to talk with and hug our friends and guests before leaving the sanctuary. One couple, whose marriage took place after they had both been widowed, included their previous spouse's mothers in their wedding ceremony. The women lit the two side candles from which the bride and groom lit the unity candle. However, after lighting the unity candle, Marilyn and Bob did not extinguish the other two, but left them lit indicating that the lives and influence of their previous spouses and families would go on into the new marriage.

The vows and the pronouncement of the commitment to one another are the essential elements of the marriage and should be in grand evidence. This is what you have asked your family and friends to witness. Choosing Scripture that has been meaningful to you as a couple is a nice touch, or selecting familiar Scripture passages about love and marriage. The passage in Genesis 2 about God's creation of man and woman and his pleasure with them and his direction about their becoming one flesh is read at many weddings, as is 1 Corinthians 13 (the "love chapter").

Gary Hanson, the young pastor who married us, had been in the same Covenant Group that I had been in for a couple of years, so I had become very close with him and his wife, Beth. His meditation for us included personal references to both of us and how he had known us in and through the church; but even more than that, it was a testimony to our love for each other and for God, as well as Christ's love for us. We asked our guests to share in the breaking of the bread and drinking of the cup with us.

One couple who married in New York State had a time in their wedding ceremony where anyone who wished could say a few words about the couple. That might be a risk at some weddings.

The Music

Music has always been an integral part of my life. Dawn, my good friend and the matron of honor in our wedding, is a coloratura soprano, so I asked her to also sing. She helped me choose the music. One of the pieces that I always loved when we sang it as a choir is "The Gift of Love," taken from 1 Corinthians 13. Dawn also sang "The Sabbath Prayer" from "Fiddler on the Roof," making a minor change or two in the lyrics to make it fit our wedding. It was lovely.

I attended a midlife wedding recently (first marriage for

the bride, second for the groom) that was such a blessing I want to tell about it. The groom had a brain tumor removed some months prior to the wedding. His prognosis was not good—he might never walk or talk again. But we mere mortals do not know and understand the power of God and the power of love. His bride-to-be steadfastly loved him and went ahead with the wedding arrangements.

On their wedding day he walked out from the side door and climbed three steps to the altar. He carefully spoke his vows, and hand in hand they descended the steps to the rousing strains of "Our God Is an Awesome God," a fitting tribute to God's healing power in this man's life and to the power of Lynn's love for her man.

The Vows

I was certain this time—and would not be swayed—that traditional wedding vows would be repeated. I wanted to say "love and obey" and mean it with all my heart. I wanted to say "for richer, for poorer, in sickness and in health, as long as we both shall live" and mean it.

Couples still write their own vows, a holdover perhaps from the weddings of the sixties when it seemed everyone wrote their own vows, promising to stay in the marriage "as long as we both shall love."

What do you want your ceremony to represent? Think about what you want those assembled to witness your vows to hear about you and about God.

The Photographs

Many couples who remarry have snapshots taken at their weddings rather than formal photographs done by professionals. In our case, my son Stephen was a budding amateur photographer who took photos at our wedding as well as at a couple of prewedding parties.

Marilyn and Bob had an amateur photographer take pictures of the wedding guests as they came out of the sanctuary. Marilyn keeps an album that includes a photo of everyone who attended their wedding. When Bob, who did not know all of her friends and relatives, asks about someone, Marilyn can show him the photo.

The Reception

First weddings often have lavish receptions that cost mountains of money. Our reception was held in the church's social hall, with all of the women from my Bible study group acting as hostesses and servers.

I baked small banana breads and fixed huge bowls of fresh fruit to serve. Rather than a wedding cake I ordered petit fours from our local bakery and had them decorated with peach rosebuds. It was simple but lovely, and there was no long-term debt involved.

One remarried bride said she made individual banana cakes for their wedding reception. Another, a skilled cake decorator, did her own wedding cake—a gorgeous pastel creation.

Gifts and Thank-You Notes

We specifically requested that no one give us wedding gifts; there was *nothing* we needed! Our request fell on deaf ears, however, and we did receive gifts and household accessories that have been precious to us over the years and have helped us remember our friends in Minnesota.

Many people who remarry in midlife will already have household goods and may not need to register in their local department stores for wedding gifts. They will probably discourage, as I did, anyone giving a bridal shower. However, it is perfectly all right if you do want a bridal shower and a friend wants to give one for you. Perhaps you do need new sheets and towels to begin your new marriage. Or perhaps you'd like to have new dishes that are not reminiscent of your previous marriage.

One nice idea someone used in lieu of wedding gifts was

to ask that if guests desired to give a gift they give to a missionary, a friend of the couple, who had a special need.

Thank you notes can be imprinted to match wedding invitations or they can be simple store-bought cards. One couple had a postcard made of one of their wedding pictures and wrote their thank you note on the back. One couple reversed their thank you notes; he sent the messages for gifts from her friends and she sent the notes for gifts from his friends. Thank you notes, in any case should be written and mailed as quickly as possible after the wedding.

Whatever you decide about your wedding and your reception, have fun.

After Every Wedding Comes a Marriage

"Ten years! I can hardly believe it," I said, on the occasion of our tenth anniversary. "Shall we have a go at ten more?"

Each anniversary we have talked in fun about whether or not to renew our marriage contract for another year. Though our marriage commitment is forever, living for the shorter term seems to make it easier—one day at a time. How are you going to ensure that you and your spouse keep coming back for one more year?

The world we live in is not strong on commitment. Husband-wife authors Bernice and Morton Hunt say it this way: "The years of mid-life are now too many, too full of promise, to be wasted, and a marriage that has become unrewarding or unsatisfying is a poisoned milieu in which the partners wither and shrivel rather than flourish and expand."[2]

In other words, quit. Give up. That's the easy way out. The world has a "throw-away" mentality: If it doesn't feel good, or it isn't useful to us, we get rid of it. Unfortunately, many midlife Christians have also bought this lie from the world and have begun the search for another marriage partner.

Is there a successful formula for a "perfect marriage"? If there is, so far no one has come forth with examples or had it packaged.

My conclusion is that commitment in a marriage is based strictly on attitude. It's the everyday commitment of two imperfect people in a relationship created by God for the good of both of them that gives stability in marriage.

I want to stay married to my husband. We are together because God brought us together. He has a purpose in our marriage. I'm committed to making it work no matter what! No strings attached! No loopholes! There is no Plan B in my marriage.

"Nothing will help a couple resolve problems sooner than their determination to stay married," reports Dr. Richard Dobbins, founder of Emerge Ministries, Inc., a Christian counseling service in Akron, Ohio, "especially when both partners are believers." The Bible makes it clear that "one flesh" is the plan after marriage. That is an *inter*dependent relationship—not one partner being overly dependent on the other nor overly independent of the other.

Your remarriage will not be without problems. No marriage is. Most problems begin to emerge after the honeymoon phase, a period that can last a few months or as long as several years. Then reality sets in, and we begin to see one another "for better or for worse." "Worse" is often the greatest test in marriage relationships—revealing but not necessarily negative.

Ten years after Bud and I said "I do" to each other, we still have problems, but not insurmountable problems. My memory is probably as selective as anyone else's, but I can still remember the first time (or what I remember as the first time) that I saw a different side of Bud from what he had shown me during our courting days.

I had made a "Honey Do" list for him, things that I wanted him to do for me in the house such as hang this lamp, put up the traverse rods, move this or that thing. When I presented him with the list (which in truth had probably grown by two or three items each day for a couple of weeks), he crumpled the list and said, "Don't ever write another list like this."

The honeymoon was over.

Changes were taking place in both of us. I was encroaching on his time and his way of doing things. We were able to talk about it and resolve the best way for me to ask him for help. Nevertheless, things had changed.

Many couples fail to realize that changes are taking place every day in their marriages. One day they look back and see that something has slipped, and they begin to be discontented and long for "the good old days"—whatever they were.

"The lofty ideas of marriage assure us that it will involve strife and conflict," writes Christian author Philip Yancey. "In marriage we are tiptoeing through a field of land mines on the way to paradise."[3]

It's going to involve change. Marriage cannot grow without change. Change hurts and requires adjustments by both marriage partners. Those years when I headed up a sales promotion department I was aware of change every day. Different fashions, different styles, new fabrics, and even in our department different techniques to improve the quality of our catalogs and TV commercials. We tried to stay on top of things. We had regular staff meetings and planning sessions so that we would always be "forward" in our thinking.

Why don't we do that in marriage? Every couple should sit down at least once a year in a quiet place and talk about where they've been, where they are, and where they're going—planning a good marriage. Anticipate the changes that are coming in your life: perhaps retirement, a scheduled surgery, the marriage of a child, a new grandchild, any event in your marriage or in your family that will make change necessary. Hard times and changes can bring a family closer together or they can rip it apart.

The mark of a successful marriage is not necessarily one where there is no conflict (if there *is* a marriage with no conflict). Rather, the successful marriage can be found where couples work to resolve the conflict in healthy ways.

It seems, however, that as human animals, we spend an inordinate amount of energy working to avoid change. Yet those couples who are open to change have the marriages most likely to survive and even grow from the stresses that are almost certain in every marriage.

"The prime purpose of this life is to know God and to be conformed to the image of His Son," writes author Carole Mayhall. "When we grasp the deep, vital truth that God achieves His purposes largely through trials and temptations, then we can 'welcome them as friends.'"[4]

But we don't like to think about that. No one ever prays "O Lord, send problems." But the Word of God promises that as we revel in his richness, we will also be subjected to prickly-pear problems, perhaps even suffering. Remember that most problems are cleverly disguised as opportunities to grow; then when your husband or wife gives you static on something, grin and say to yourself, "Here is an opportunity to grow."

Love

"What relationships need is love," writes popular radio teacher and pastor Charles Swindoll.

[It is] what husbands need with wives, and parents with children, and wives with husbands, bosses with employees, and fellow members of the family of God with business relations. It is love. It is the essential ingredient. It isn't optional. Remove it and you have reduced life to a grinding, irksome, friction-filled series of demands and requirements and sterile assignments. . . . Take it away and you have zero.[5]

Say "I love you" often. Never assume that your mate knows how you feel. The guy who says, "I said I love you once. I'll let you know when I change my mind," isn't funny. Men and women alike need to hear words of love regularly.

Praying for your mate is one of the most loving things you can do. A devotion I read one morning brought home the truth of the power of prayer. The woman was ready to divorce her husband, because in a moment of anger he had slapped her. He was genuinely sorry and asked her to forgive him. She refused. She also declared that she no longer loved him. But she went to see a counselor who called her attention to Titus 2:4, which admonishes "the younger women to love their husbands."

The counselor assured her that if she would start praying for her husband and would treat him with kindness she would fall in love with him again. She accepted the challenge. Her love for him was restored and so was their marriage.

"Somehow a husband and wife have to learn to communicate a love that stretches around any bulges of failure and disappointment," says Philip Yancey. "Love and acceptance are not rubber bands that weaken as they are stretched; they become stronger as they are tested and the partner perceives trust and faithful love."[6]

Acceptance

Husbands and wives are often shocked to discover how differently they see things, think about things.

One woman had spent weeks ministering to a sick loved one. She expressed the distance she felt between herself and her husband. "He went along with business as usual, while I was a wreck worrying about losing a family member."

She discovered later, though, that her husband had made a point to keep life as normal as possible precisely because she was so distressed. It was actually his way of showing support, not indifference. They had handled the problem in different ways.

As I complete this manuscript, I am aware that my house has not been thoroughly cleaned since last fall, there are bags of tulip and hyacinth bulbs that have probably rotted because they weren't planted when they should have been, and probably lots of other things I am responsible for that are not done. By the same token, I could think of things I wish my husband would do. But none of those things were on the agenda when we stood at the front of that big church in Minneapolis and joined our lives. All I know is that God gave this man to me and me to Bud to honor and cherish and enjoy. Rather than fret about those things that my husband is not, I am choosing to celebrate what he is.

Crisis Proof Your Marriage

Marital problems do not evaporate. In fact, they accumulate. Ignoring them leads to what Sheldon Vanauken called creeping separateness. He describes it as the insidious time when *we* and *our* turns into *I* and *mine*. Self once again becomes the focus: What do *I* want to do?

Better to face down the problems. Counseling helps. But many couples wait and wait until their marriage situation is so bad that no counselor could possibly sort through the hurts, the anger, the disappointments.

If your marriage is not satisfying, do not wait. If you and your new spouse cannot settle an issue through communication and prayer, then make a date to see a counselor. If your spouse is not willing to go, then go alone. Even if only one of you receives counsel, you may be able to change or improve a situation at home.

My experience is that when one person in a marriage makes an important change in attitude or behavior, the other members of the family must, by necessity, also change. Here are some ideas that may help you to prepare.

Reserve time for each other every day.

Express love and appreciation daily.

Keep a clean slate. Talk about your small problems and solve them daily if possible.

Seek forgiveness for wrongs and grant it quickly.

Stay flexible. Keep your routines adaptable to change.

Find out what your partner thinks. Learn to deal with conflict by using "what if" questions. "What if we had to move because of your job?" "What if my arthritis makes me unable to work?"

Pray about everything.

The vain regrets of yesterday
Have vanished through God's pardoning grace;
The guilty fear has passed away,
And joy has come to take its place.

Ackley

Remarriage can be a happy place where the two of you are free to be everything God wants you to be. Rather than marrying for better or for worse, marry for good. From here on it's up to you.

Notes

Chapter 1. Changes and Challenges in Midlife

1. Bernice Hunt, Morton Hunt, *Prime Time* (New York: Stein and Day Publishers, 1975), 184.

2. "Two-thirds of Marriages will 'Disrupt'" *Spartanburg Journal,* Spartanburg, S.C., March 9, 1989.

3. "Divorce Loses" *Psychology Today,* September 1988, 8.

4. Charles Leerhsen, Deborah Witherspoon, Tenley-Ann Jackson, "I Do, I Do, I Do" *Newsweek,* October 7, 1985, 84.

5. Derek Prince, *God Is a Matchmaker* (Old Tappan, N.J.: Fleming H. Revell Company, 1986), 143.

Chapter 2. Help from the Top

1. Derek Prince, *God Is a Matchmaker* (Old Tappan, N.J.: Fleming H. Revell Company, 1986), 140.

2. Delores Kuenning, *Helping People Through Grief* (Minneapolis: Bethany House Publishers, 1987), 148.

3. Ibid., 213.

4. Prince, *God Is a Matchmaker,* 131.

5. Guy Duty, *Divorce & Remarriage* (Minneapolis: Bethany Fellowship, Inc., 1967), 16.

6. Edward G. Dobson, *What The Bible Really Says About Marriage, Divorce and Remarriage* (Old Tappan, N.J.: Fleming H. Revell Company, 1986), 41.

7. Ibid., 60.

8. Ibid., 67.

9. Ibid., 81.

10. W. E. Vine, *An Expository Dictionary of New Testament Words* (Chicago: Moody Press, 1988), 246.

11. Elisabeth Elliott, *Through Gates of Splendor* (Wheaton, Ill.: Tyndale House Publishers, Inc., December, 1988), 53.

Chapter 3. From Wreckage to Renewal

1. Mary Kay Blakely, "After Divorce" (Quote of the Week) *Parade Magazine*, July 12, 1987, 7.

2. Dale E. Galloway, *Dream a New Dream; How to Rebuild a Broken Life* (Wheaton, Ill.: Tyndale House Publishers, Inc., 1975), 44.

3. Ibid., 49.

4. Bud and Kathy Pearson, *Single Again: Remarrying for the Right Reason* (Ventura, Calif.: Regal Books, 1985).

5. Robin Norwood, *Women Who Love Too Much* (Los Angeles: Jeremy P. Tarcher, Inc., 1985), 183.

6. Robert Subby, *Lost in the Shuffle* (Deerfield Beach, Fla.: Health Communications, Inc., 1987), 20.

Chapter 4. An Ounce of Prevention Is Still Worth a Pound of Cure

1. Holly Hall, "Marriage: Practice Makes Imperfect?" *Psychology Today*, July 1988, 15.

2. Ibid.

3. Bernice and Morton Hunt, *Prime Time* (New York: Stein and Day, Publishers, 1975), 190.

4. Adeline McDonnell, Beverly Anderson, *Single After 50* (New York: McGraw-Hill Book Company, 1978), 265.

5. Ibid., 266.

Chapter 5. Marrying the Multitudes: Secondary Relationships

1. David Field, *Family Personalities* (Eugene, Oreg.: Harvest House Publishers, 1988), 12.

2. Ibid., 135.

3. Emily and John Visher, *How to Win as a Stepfamily* (New York: Dembner Book, 1982)

Chapter 6. Step Relationships: Adult to Adult

1. Margaret Doren, in June Noble, *How to Live With Other People's Children* (New York: Hawthorn Books, Inc., 1977), 99.

2. "Children of the Aftershock" *Newsweek*, February 6, 1989, 61.

3. Judith Wallerstein, *Second Chances* (New York: Ticknor & Fields, 1989), 299.

4. *Webster's New World Dictionary*, Third College Edition (New York: Simon & Schuster, Inc., 1988).

5. Leslie Aldridge Westoff, *Second Time Around* (New York: Viking Press, 1977), 82.

6. Mary Lou Fuller, "Facts and Fictions About Stepfamilies" *Education Digest*, October 1988, 53.

7. Ibid.

8. Ibid.

9. Ibid.

10. *Webster's New World Dictionary*, Third College Edition (New York: Simon & Schuster, Inc., 1988).

11. Florence Littauer, *Silver Boxes* (Dallas: Word Publishing, 1989), 4.

12. Elizabeth Skoglund, *Growing Through Rejection* (Wheaton, Ill.: Tyndale House Publishers, Inc., 1983), 59.

Chapter 7. Expect Problems

1. Emily B. and John S. Visher, *Stepfamilies: A Guide to Working With Stepparents and Stepchildren* (New York: Brunnel/Mazar, Inc., 1979), 261–267.

2. Bobbie Reed, *Stepfamilies Living in Christian Harmony* (St. Louis: Concordia Publishing House, 1980), 65.

3. Brenda Maddox, *The Half Parent* (New York: Evans, 1975), 65.

4. Elizabeth Einstein, *The Stepfamily: Living, Loving and Learning* (Boston: Shambhala Publications, 1982).

5. Gerald L. Dahl, *Why Christian Marriages Are Breaking Up* (Nashville: Thomas Nelson Publishers, 1979), 16.

Chapter 8. Bonding the Primary Relationship

1. David Hocking, *Marrying Again: A Guide for Christians* (Old Tappan, N.J.: Fleming H. Revell Company, 1983), 152.

2. Tom Anderson, "How Love Came Back" *Guideposts*, August 1985.

3. Ken Abraham, *Unmasking the Myths of Marriage* (Old Tappan, N.J.: Fleming H. Revell Company, 1990), 34.

4. Leo Buscaglia, "How to Make Love Grow" *Reader's Digest*, February 1985, 77.

5. Ken Abraham, *Unmasking the Myths of Marriage* (Old Tappan, N.J.: Fleming H. Revell Company, 1990), 25.

Chapter 9. Handling Hurts

1. Larry Crabb, *Inside Out* (Colorado Springs: NavPress, 1988), 116.

2. Traci Mullins, "Friendship: The Essence of Life," *Aglow*, July/August 1988, 19.

3. Elizabeth Skoglund, *Growing Through Rejection* (Wheaton, Ill.: Tyndale House Publishers, Inc., 1983), 44.

4. Lewis B. Smedes, *Forgive and Forget* (San Francisco: Harper and Row, 1984), 133

5. Ibid., 139.
6. Ibid., 27.

Chapter 10. Holidays: Rest or Ruin?

1. Giampiero Bartolucci, in Gary R. Collins, *Coping With Christmas* (Minneapolis: Bethany Fellowship, Inc., 1975), 8.
2. Ann Hibbard, *Family Celebrations* (Brentwood, Tenn.: Wolgemuth & Hyatt, Publishers, Inc., 1988), 2.
3. Gary R. Collins, *Coping With Christmas* (Minneapolis: Bethany Fellowship, Inc. 1975), 31.
4. Paul Tournier, *The Meaning of Gifts* (Richmond, Va.: John Knox Press, 1963), 28.

Chapter 11. For Richer or Poorer

1. David Hocking, *Marrying Again: A Guide for Christians* (Old Tappan, N.J.: Fleming H. Revell Company, 1983), 79.
2. Kevin McManus, "Love & Money" *Changing Times,* July 1988, 21-30.
3. Leslie Aldridge Westoff, *The Second Time Around: Remarriage in America* (New York: Viking Press, 1977), 55.
4. Charles E. Cohen, "The Double Jeopardies of Blended Families" *Money,* March 1989, 77.
5. Claire Berman, *Making It As a Stepparent* (Garden City: Doubleday, 1980), 164.
6. Ibid., 162.
7. John G. Watts, *Leave Your House in Order* (Wheaton, Ill.: Tyndale House Publishers, Inc., 1979), 22.
8. Ibid., 23.
9. Ibid., 82.

Chapter 12. In Sickness and in Health

1. Arthur J. Norton, Bureau of Census, in Bernice and Morton Hunt, *Prime Time* (New York: Stein and Day Publishers, 1975), 192.
2. Redford Williams, "Your Anger Can Kill You" *Reader's Digest* (August 1989), 184.
3. Melinda Blau, "Caregiving: Coping with a Chronically Ill Spouse" *McCall's* (November 1989), 108, 110.
4. Ibid., 108.

Chapter 13. Parenting Our Parents

1. Amanda Lloyd, "Parenting Your Parents" *Today's Christian Woman,* March/April 1989, 38.

2. Elaine Cohen, director of Pathfinders/Eldercare, Scarsdale, New York. Used with permission.

3. Shirley Flanagan, "Caring for the Elderly at Home" *Home Life*, November 1981, 44.

4. Ibid., 46.

5. Eric Schurenberg, "The Crunch of Caring for Both Parents and Kids" *Money*, March 1989, 93.

6. Bette McCaulley, "Caring for Aging Parents Is Stressful" *USA Today*, May 1988, 11.

7. Marilyn Fanning, "A Glimpse of God" *Today's Christian Woman*, March/April 1989, 43.

8. Patricia H. Rushford, "Guilt . . . Guilt . . . Guilt" *Today's Christian Woman*, March/April 1989, 41.

Chapter 14. Dream a New Dream

1. Myrna and Robert Kysar, *The Asundered* (Atlanta: John Knox Press, 1978), 104.

2. Bernice and Morton Hunt, *Prime Time* (New York: Stein and Day Publishers, 1975), 186.

3. Philip Yancey, "Wading Through Marital Conflicts" *Focus on the Family*, April 1985, 14.

4. Carole Mayhall, *Filled to Overflowing* (Colorado Springs: NavPress, 1984), 97–107.

5. Charles R. Swindoll, "What Makes Relationships Work?" *Insights*, Winter 1982, 3.

6. Philip Yancey, "Wading Through Marital Conflicts" *Focus on the Family*, April 1985, 14.

Suggestions for Further Reading

Chapter 1. Changes and Challenges in Midlife

God Is a Matchmaker, Derek Prince, A Chosen Book, Fleming H. Revell Company, Old Tappan, N.J., 1986.

Before You Remarry, H. Norman Wright, Harvest House Publishers, Eugene, Oreg., 1988.

Remarriage & God's Renewing Grace, Dwight Hervey Small, Baker Book House, Grand Rapids, 1986.

Chapter 2. Help from the Top

Helping People Through Grief, Delores Kuenning, Bethany House Publishers, Minneapolis, 1987.

What The Bible Really Says About Marriage, Divorce and Remarriage, Edward G. Dobson, Fleming H. Revell Company, Old Tappan, N.J., 1986.

Chapter 3. From Wreckage to Renewal

Telling Yourself the Truth, William Backus and Marie Chapian, Bethany House Publishers, Minneapolis, 1980.

Christ Esteem, Don Matzat, Harvest House Publishers, Eugene, Oreg., 1990.

Chapter 4. An Ounce of Prevention Is Still Worth a Pound of Cure

Personality Plus, Florence Littauer, Fleming H. Revell Company, Old Tappan, N.J., 1982.

Chapter 5. Marrying the Multitudes: Secondary Relationships

Family Personalities, David Field, Harvest House Publishers, Eugene, Oreg., 1988.

Marriage Personalities, David Field, Harvest House Publishers, Eugene, Oreg., 1986.

Chapter 6. Step Relationships: Adult to Adult

Growing Through Rejection, Elizabeth Skoglund, Tyndale House
Publishers, Inc. Wheaton, Ill., 1983.

Silver Boxes, Florence Littauer, Word Publishing, Dallas, 1989.

Chapter 7. Expect Problems

Love Must Be Tough, James Dobson, Word Publishing, Dallas, 1986.

Chapter 8. Bonding the Primary Relationship

Marrying Again: A Guide for Christians, David Hocking, Power Books,
Fleming H. Revell Company, Old Tappan, N.J., 1983.

Unmasking the Myths of Marriage, Ken Abraham, Fleming H. Revell
Company, Old Tappan, N.J., 1990

Chapter 9. Handling Hurts

Forgive and Forget, Lewis B. Smedes, Harper and Row, San Francisco,
1984.

Inside Out, by Larry Crabb, NavPress, Colorado Springs, 1988.

Chapter 10. Holidays: Rest or Ruin?

Family Celebrations, Ann Hibbard, Wolgemuth & Hyatt, Publishers,
Inc., Nashville, 1988.

Let's Make a Memory, Shirley Dobson and Gloria Gaither, Word
Publishing, Dallas, 1986.

Prime Time Together . . . With Kids, Donna Erickson, Augsburg,
Minneapolis, 1989.

Chapter 11. For Richer or Poorer

Leave Your House in Order, John G. Watts, Tyndale House Publishers,
Inc., Wheaton, Ill., 1979.

Chapter 13. Parenting Our Parents

As Our Years Increase, Tim Stafford, Zondervan Publishing House,
Grand Rapids, Mich., 1989.

You Can Enjoy Your Aging Parents, Margaret J. Anderson, Concordia
Publishing House, St. Louis, 1979.

Chapter 14. Dream a New Dream

Growing a Great Marriage, Bob and Emilie Barnes, Harvest House
Publishers, Eugene, Oreg., 1988.

Your Marriage Can Survive Mid-Life Crisis, Jim and Sally Conway,
Thomas Nelson, Nashville, 1987.